I0027258

The Census Tables

for the

French Colony of Louisiana

From 1699 Through 1732

The Census Tables

for the

French Colony of Louisiana

From 1699 Through 1732

Compiled and translated by

CHARLES R. MADUELL, JR.
*New Orleans, Louisiana*

CLEARFIELD

Copyright © 1972
Genealogical Publishing Company, Inc.
Baltimore, Maryland
All Rights Reserved.

Reprinted for
Clearfield Company by
Genealogical Publishing Co.
Baltimore, Maryland
1993, 1995, 2000, 2003, 2008

Library of Congress Catalogue Card Number 72-1355
ISBN-13: 978-0-8063-0490-8
ISBN 10: 0-8063-0490-1

*Made in the United States of America*

# INTRODUCTION

In April of the year 1682 Robert Cavalier, Sieur de la Salle, discovered the delta of the Mississippi River after travelling down the river from Illinois Indian country. Except for an aborted attempt in 1685 to find the river and establish a colony, the only result of which was the murder of Robert Cavalier by his own men, the French did little in Louisiana.

Pierre de la Moine, Sieur d'Iberville, left France for Louisiana in September, 1698 with the objective of carrying out the plans of Sieur de la Salle. With him was his brother, Jean Baptiste de la Moine, Sieur de Bienville, who was destined to play the greatest role of any individual toward establishing a French colony on the coast of the Gulf of Mexico. This colony later expanded to the Mississippi River.

Iberville and Bienville established their first colonies in the islands bordering the Gulf Coast. These included Isle Massacre, now Dauphin Island near Mobile and Ship Island near Biloxi.

Little colonial development occurred, however, since Bienville was preoccupied with the matter of attempting to capture and hold the Spanish fort at Pensacola. As a consequence, little in the way of colonization was accomplished. Yet the period between 1699 and 1712 did witness the establishment of Biloxi, Mobile, and some islands, as well as explorations of the Mississippi River, some of its lower tributaries, and the lakes, which would become of importance in the future.

There are in existence several lists of names of Frenchmen who were responsible for these early explorations and colonizations. Most are lists of soldiers whom we cannot call colonists, since many either died in the Indian and Spanish wars of the period, or returned to France after their term of service was over. Others have indexed these military lists[1] and therefore they are not of concern in this manuscript.

Other lists such as those of persons desiring to migrate to Louisiana, muster rolls and passenger lists are available, but not all persons on these lists ever saw the shores of America.

One does find in the census of Fort Maurepas dated December, 1699 the names of some persons destined to continue activity in the colony for many years. Comparing this list with that of May, 1700 for Biloxi, we find many of these still active in the colony. Some remained even thirty years later. To mention a few, we find Gravline, Tesserontierre (possibly a form of Tixerand), Le Vasseur, St. Denis, Belair, La Pointe, and the Chauvin brothers, Minet, Trepanier, Montreuil, and Roussel.

Among the earliest settlers was Nicolas de la Salle, the nephew of Robert Cavalier and a witness to his murder. To him we attribute Louisiana's first census, that of August 1, 1706, two forms of this census, one which lists only the inhabitants of Mobile, the other listing the civilian population of the entire colony.

A map of Mobile in 1711 gives more information, but this was several years

---

[1]Winston de Ville, Louisiana Troops, 1720 - 1770 (Fort Worth 1965)

after the census of Nicolas de la Salle. This was also during the time when, because of flooding, Mobile was rebuilt upriver from its original site, in its present location.

In September, 1712 a charter was given to Antoine Crozat to develop the colony of Louisiana as a commercial venture. The period between the initiation of this charter and its dissolution, August, 1717, marked no serious attempts at a census. The only way we have to determine who was in the colony is by comparison of early tables with later tables, or to refer to letters and memoranda from Crozat's directors to the public officials in France. Letters from Duclos, d'Artaguette, and others duplicate information given in the letters of the governor, LaMothe Cadillac. The letters, in translated form, are available in libraries in Washington, D.C., Jackson, Mississippi, New Orleans, Louisiana, and other places.[2]

The principal content of these letters seems to consist of accusations against Bienville. Throughout the period Bienville appears to have made enemies of Nicolas de la Salle, Cadillac, de la Chaise, and Perier. He was vindicated by Duclos, d'Artaguiette, and others, but the conflict of personality is well established in these letters.

Crozat's regime saw the establishment of Louisiana's first town, Natchitoches, Mississippi's second town, Fort Rosalie, now Natchez, and also an event which changed the history of the colony, the death of King Louis XIV.

The regency of the Duke of Orleans was the beginning of a more serious attempt to make a paying colony out of Louisiana. The beginnings were the establishment of the Western Company, soon to be called the Mississippi Company, and finally, the Company of the Indies. This company was established in August, 1717 and took over Crozat's charter. Yet, serious immigration into Louisiana did not occur until 1719. There are a large number of passenger lists of persons embarking from La Rochelle, and later l'Orient for Louisiana between 1718 and 1722. Some of these lists have been transcribed by others[3,4] but to a large extent, the several thousand (some say as many as 6,000) persons who were sent to the colony did not all survive, and their names are little more than entries on obsolete passenger lists.

In the meantime, the most important town on the Mississippi River, New Orleans, was established (1718). Bienville, since his first explorations of the river with his brother in the earlier years, had tried to promote this dream.

The censuses of 1721 and 1722 show the first colonists at New Orleans, the villages along the river near the city, Biloxi, Mobile, and along the Gulf Coast, and plantations or concessions along the Mississippi River including Natchez. They also include Natchitoches. These census tables are principally the work

---

[2] Dunbar Rowland, Mississippi Provincial Archives, in three volumes, Vols. II and III are principally concerned with the translations of letters to and from France by various persons, and are part of the files C 13 of the Archives des Colonies.

[3] Victor Tantet, Passenger Lists, hand transcribed from the original documents. A copy is in the Louisiana Museum Library, St. Ann at Chartres Street, New Orleans, Louisiana.

[4] Winston de Ville, Louisiana Colonials, Soldiers and Vagabonds, Genealogical Publishing Company (Baltimore 1963).

of Sieur Diron (d'Artaguiette), an official in the colony during these times.

Not everyone is named in the census. Certain exceptions such as women who bear the name of their husbands, children who bear the name of their fathers, and engagees, people of European descent who were domestic servants of those who were established on the concessions, are not named. Many of these engagees are named in other census tables at a later date when the plantations began to dissolve and the engagees established autonomy. Also not named are the soldiers who probably returned to France after their term of service had expired.

In the early 1720s Bienville had been ordered back to France. However, he was still in the colony until 1725. His authority as governor had been given to Serigny, with du Sauvoy and de la Chaise as Ordinators. These men, with Perier and Perault, were in control of the colony until Bienville's return in 1732.

The era between 1718 and 1725 was the period of the great concessions along the river, with that at Natchez, controlled by M. Kolly, the most prosperous. Indigo and tobacco were the commodities of the plantations, but the cultivation of the former was not too successful.

There are 1,040 individuals named in the census tables of 1721 through 1725. An additional 455 are mentioned but not named, since they are the engagees. There are in addition about 1,000 women and children, also not named in these census tables, indicating a total population of about 2,500 persons of European descent. Negroes and Indian slaves are also prominent in the colony. They are not named since only Christian given names were used by these persons.

De la Chaise wrote two lengthy letters during 1723. In these he established for the French officials in Paris those who were important in the colony during this period.[2] Names extracted from these letters are also transcribed by this writer in separate tables.

John Law had sent a large number of Germans from Alsace and the Rhine Valley to his concession on the Arkansas River. These Germans, dissatisfied with the lack of materials and cooperation from their overseers, decided to request their passage back to France. Instead, they were given land of their own at a place henceforth called des Allemands, ten leagues from New Orleans and on the left bank (ascending) of the river. For the first time except in the shipping passenger lists[5] we have the names of the survivors of the engagees sent to Louisiana. The names are listed in the census of 1724 under the command of le Sieur d'Arensbourg, himself either a Swiss officer or a German, depending on the source of information. Hanno Deiler[6] has given us a translation of these names into their original and final "American" form, but the French census reporters were not careful to preserve these names for us in their original spellings. These names were for the most part spelled in the phonetic French of the period.

It is to be noted, that the French gave the German engagees land on the left bank of the river, which they thought to be a useless swamp, while retaining for themselves the land along the right bank. This is indicated in another census of 1724.

---

[5]Alice D. Forsyth and Erlene L. Zeringue, German Pest Ships, Genealogical Research Society of New Orleans (New Orleans 1969).

[6]J. Hanno Deiler, The Settlement of the German Coast of Louisiana and the Creoles of German Descent, Genealogical Publishing Company (Baltimore 1970).

A short census of 1725 for the islands, indicates how the sand dunes of Dauphin, Cat, and the river banks of the Mobile River and the Pascagoula swamp had been depopulated.

Perier, Governor of Louisiana from 1726 to 1731, is responsible for giving researchers in Louisiana history the most nearly complete census for the first thirty years of Louisiana history. The colony now included the lands along the Mississippi River not only from its mouth to Natchez, but the former colony of Illinois as well. This census shows several advantages over previous ones, and although only about 1,000 names are found, they represent 1,952 persons of European origin, with only 276 persons remaining unnamed in these pages. Thus, most of the engagees who were still living in 1726, and not named in previous records, are now to be accounted for.

Although still not a profitable venture, Louisiana was established. New Orleans had moved from an unimportant village to the principal village of the colony. The farms up and down the river, the village of Natchez, the Illinois country, Natchitoches and Mobile were important towns. The islands had lost population except for a few sturdy individuals who remained. They would be the first to observe any ships coming to the colony.

Indian slaves had proven to be uneconomical. European engagees were settled on their own lands. The colony required workers to make the concessions profitable. They now demanded the Company of the Indies send them Negroes to do the work.

Bienville himself, in a letter to the administrators in France, had often complained that Indians were useless except as hunters and fishermen. They often escaped when required to work, but Negroes would not be familiar with the land and would not find it easy to escape. The most prominent citizens of Louisiana who requested Negroes are listed in another of the tables in this thesis.

Perier is responsible for another census in 1727, only a year and a half from the preceding census. This one does not include Mobile, the Gulf Coast Islands, Biloxi, Natchitoches, or Illinois. Yet it does list the part of the colony most important to the company, New Orleans and the plantations along the river. Comparison with the preceding census shows how that part of the colony grew in this year and a half.

The end of the colony at Natchez came during November, 1729 when the Indians decided to get the French out of Louisiana by a planned and successful massacre. Fortunately for the French, the Indians were not joined by the other tribes of the Choctaw nations, and the colony continued in its other sections. Out of the 2,000 or so Europeans in Louisiana, from Mobile to Natchitoches, and from La Balize to Illinois, some 200 were killed at Natchez.

As a result of this massacre, Bienville was recalled to the governorship of the colony, and temporary command was given to Gatien Salmon as Ordinator. The colony at Natchez was not replaced until much later when the east bank of the Mississippi River was given to the English as a war prize in the 1760s.

The city of New Orleans had been planned by several architects, among whom de la Tour and de Pauger were the most important. Later the position of Royal Engineer went to Baron and to Broutin, who were employees of Pauger. The city had been laid out on a square pattern, but only extended several blocks in each direction. One of the engineer draftsmen, Gonichon, made a map in 1731, on the margin of which he located the buildings and their proprietors. This map contains a list of those who owned the property but not those who lived in the house. Many of the property owners had returned to France by this time, leaving maintenance of the property to the Superior Council.

In 1731 and 1732 more censuses were taken, these being unsigned but initialled "N. S." One does not find these initials in the tables, but since this was the period between the recall of Perier and the reappearance of Bienville, one can assume these tables were generated for Salmon.

The first of these is a census of inhabitants and proprietors along the banks of the river, up to and including the place called Pointe Coupee. This area is on the Louisiana side of the Mississippi River, and is to this day called by the same name. It is just opposite the present limit of the Louisiana-Mississippi state line.

The second of these census tables includes the city of New Orleans, showing property owners (proprietors) and residents of the city. One can compare this census with the preceding ones (1726 - 1727) and will find that the population within the city has dropped considerably due principally to the Natchez massacre and the subsequent return to France of many of the prominent citizens of previous decades.

The trend to return to France is indicated in the next table, which lists landowners along the river, and how they acquired their land. It is noted that much land was sold to new owners, adjacent property owners, tenants, and the like before the promised Indian attack. This attack never took place. We note that the Germans did not abandon their land, and actually profited by the emigration of their French neighbors. Others married widows and gained the property in this way for their children.

The final census in this group is that of Illinois, which like New Orleans, was another stable locality due to the prospect of lead and silver mines. These commodities had been reported to Cadillac twenty years before, and left to La Sieur and Reynault to develop. Fort Chartres and Cacassias were the important areas in these places, but were much left to their own in after years.

Bienville was too preoccupied with Indian wars when he returned in 1732, so the census tabulations for the French colony of Louisiana practically ceased at that point. It makes little difference, however, since new colonists were rare, and the only ships coming to Louisiana carried principally cargo to trade for tobacco, rice, and other products from the Mississippi Valley.[7] This was the status until the 1760s when the Spanish compiled several census reports.

Charles R. Maduell, Jr.
March, 1971

My thanks to the following organizations for help provided.

The Library of Congress for the microfilms of some parts of the records from the Archives des Colonies.

The Howard Tilton Library of Tulane University for making available the references indicated on the next page.

The Louisiana Museum Library for making available the Recensements of Victor Tantet.

The New Orleans Public Library for the use of its reprints of many old maps for the area.

---

[7]John G. Clark, New Orleans 1718 - 1812, An Economic History, Louisiana State University Press (New Orleans 1969).

## GENERAL REFERENCES

Most of the information in these pages was obtained from the Library of Congress, from microfilms relating to the Manuscripts in the Archives des Colonies in Paris. The list of documents concerned with the history of the Mississippi Valley in the Archives des Colonies and other places in France is indexed in N. M. Surrey, Calendar of Manuscripts in the Paris Archives and Libraries Relating to the History of the Mississippi Valley to 1803. Vol. I, 1581-1739, Vol. II, 1740-1803. Carnegie Institute of Washington.

An historic summary of the events of the period will be found in Francois Xavier Martin, The History of Louisiana. Pelican Publishing Co. Chapters IV-XII.

## TEXT REFERENCES

AC GI indicates that the originals of the document are located in the Archives des Colonies, Paris, and copies are in the Library of Congress on microfilm. The number following is the file number.

BN indicates that the original is located in files other than in the Archives des Colonies, and in other areas in France. A copy of the document is on microfilm in the Library of Congress.

The following references, used in the List of Census Tables, are of books and articles containing translations or transcripts of the original documents, and were used in conjunction with the sources mentioned above. These materials were found in the New Orleans Public Library, The Howard Tilton Library of Tulane University and the Louisiana Museum Library in New Orleans.

Rowland. Mississippi, Heart of the South. Vol. I.

Hamilton. The Founding of Mobile.

Deep South. The Deep South Genealogical Quarterly. Vol. I, Nos. 1, 3.

Beer. Early Census Tables of Louisiana. Louisiana Historical Association publication No. IV. This contains copies of the originals of many of the documents, as interpreted by William Beer, who derived his data from Tantet.

Tantet. Recensements. Victor Tantet, of Paris, transcribed by hand, many of the census tables as well as other data. This book was given to the Louisiana Historical Society and is now in the Louisiana Museum Library. The transcription is in French and does not always agree with the originals on the microfilms from the Archives des Colonies, especially in the spelling of the names.

MPA II. Mississippi Provincial Archives. This is a collection of letters and other data from the Archives des Colonies, gathered by Dunbar Rowland and others. Three volumes contain the records from 1701 through 1729.

LHQ. The Louisiana Historical Quarterly contains a translation of some census records, cited above, principally the partial census of New Orleans for 1721, and part of the census of 1726 for New Orleans.

Bobinski. <u>Natchitoches</u>. By Germaine Portre Bobinski and Clara Mildred Smith, this work contains translations of documents relating to this area.

Deiler. <u>The Settlement of the German Coast of Louisiana and the Creoles of German Descent</u>, by J. Hanno Deiler. His translations are of some records found in Tantet, and are not always in agreement with others, as Deiler attempts to retranslate the names found in Tantet to the original German form. This does not detract from the usefulness of Deiler's work, but is rather to his credit. Deiler omits much data found in the originals, and in Tantet particularly, if it does not relate to the Germans.

# LIST OF THE CENSUS TABLES FOR THE FRENCH
## COLONY OF LOUISIANA FROM 1699 THROUGH 1732

| Table | Sources |
|---|---|
| A-99 | Census of the Inhabitants of the first settlement on the Gulf Coast, Fort Maurepas, December, 1699<br>AC C13 218 Rowland |
| A-00 | Census of the Officers, petty officers, sailors, Canadians, freebooters, and others located at Biloxi as of May 25, 1700<br>AC C13 207 Rowland |
| A-04 | List of marriageable girls who arrived aboard the Pelican at Biloxi in the year 1704<br>BN 22813 Hamilton |
| A-06 | Census of the Inhabitants of Fort Louis de la Louisianne at Mobile, taken by Nicolas de la Salle, August 1, 1706<br>AC F1 13 113 Hamilton |
| B-06 | Census of families and habitants of Louisiana taken August 1, 1706 by Nicolas de la Salle<br>AC C13 2:225 Deep South, Beer, Tantet |
| A-11 | Census of Fort Louis de la Mobile from the map of 1711<br>Hamilton |
| A-13 | List of officers commissioned at Fort Louis, Biloxi, October 25, 1713 |
| A-13 | Persons mentioned in the Colony by Antoine de la Mothe Cadillac, October 1713<br>MPA II |
| A-21 | General Census of all the inhabitants of New Orleans and environs dated November 24, 1721 as reported by Le sieur Diron<br>AC G1 464 Tantet, Beer, LHQ |
| B-21 | Census of the inhabitants in the area of Biloxi and Mobile dated June 26, 1721 as reported by Le sieur Diron<br>AC G1 464 Tantet, Deep South |
| A-22 | Census of the habitants of the concessions along the Mississippi River dated May 13, 1722 as reported by Le sieur Diron<br>AC G1 464 Tantet |
| B-22 | Census of the habitants of Natchitoches, Fort St. Jean Baptist taken for Sieur Diron, General of the Troops, May 1, 1722<br>AC G1 464 Tantet, Beer, Bobinski |
| C-22 | Officials of the colony at Fort Louis, Biloxi appointed in 1722<br>MPA II |

date mentioned "after 1731"
AC G1 464

C-32    Census of the inhabitants of Illinois dated January 1, 1732, unsigned but initialled N. S.
AC G1 464 Tantet

# FRENCH NAME PRACTICES
## IN THE
### SEVENTEENTH AND EIGHTEENTH CENTURIES

In all the cultures of western Europe, the practice of surname usage is no—
where as complex as it is in France. This is probably because France is really
the crossroads of Europe, the cultures of Latin based Italy, Teutonic based
German, Celtic based Breton, mixed with Basque, Norman, and Spanish, all
contributing to the French language.

Surnames in France were not stabilized so that the name of the father be-
came the family name. Although this practice was more or less prevailing, it
did not have legal enforcement, and a son or daughter was free to adapt the surname of his father or not, as wished.

This practice brought with it the flagrant use of the preposition "de" and the
article "le," and even the combination of preposition and article in the forms "de
la" and "des." Fortunately, there is some semblance of order in the use of these
prefixes before the more complex names.

The preposition "de" and its modified form "du" were originally used by the
nobility to denote the possession of an estate, the name of the estate following the
preposition. We find, that, as an example, three brothers whose father was
named Lemoine were prominent in Louisiana. They were the sieurs de Bienville,
d'Iberville, and de Chateaugue. We even find that the surname Lemoine was not
used, preference being for the estate name, even to the extent of dropping the
preposition.

We find this practice even among those who had little or no claim to a title.
Thus, the four Chauvin brothers, three of whom established estates along the
river above New Orleans, adopted the estate names de Lery, afterward Delery,
de la Freniere, afterward Lafreniere, and de Beaulieu, afterward Beaulieu. Of
the fourth brother little is known, but the name Chauvin was well established in
Louisiana, even in the early period.

In the census tables, which form the major part of this thesis, names beginning with the preposition "de" or "du" are often found in places where the preposition has been dropped, hence, we should look in several places for any specific
surname which may or may not have been an estate name. Thus, in the early
census we might find M. Delery under Chauvin, under De Lery, or under Lery.

The officials of Louisiana sometimes used the preposition and sometimes
not, so the reader looking for a specific name may find it in either place, or in
both places.

Unfortunately, the use of the preposition does not establish that the name
following was an estate. In some cases, the preposition takes its rightful defini-
tion, meaning "of" or "from" and the name following is a place, not necessarily
an estate. Such names as Dupont (by the bridge), Duval (from the valley), De
Belisle (from the pretty island) would be of this form. It is highly possible that
bearers of such names had other family names as well, although many may be
lost in history.

The article "la" or "le" before names is much more common among those
Frenchmen who were from the north, Normandy or Picardy. The article pre-

supposes that at one time or another the bearers' ancestors were serfs or villagers with more or less freedom but belonging to or assigned to an individual bearing the name following. Names such as Lachapelle obviously signify that the ancestor was from Chapelle, while a name such as Lavigne signifies that the ancestor worked for or belonged to M. Vigne.

It has been the practice in America to bring together the preposition or the article with the remainder of the name, thus, a name which may have once been separated, as La Place is now Laplace and Du Val is now Duval.

Carrying the practice of surnames as applying to Frenchmen even further is the use of combined preposition and article. We then notice such names as de la Chaise, or Deschamps. These have the same significance as above, but we might find the same person mentioned in several places under a different name. A good example is M. Marc Antoine de la Loire des Ursins, who appears in separate census tables with any one of his names, omitting the others.

The problem of finding specific persons in French census tables is further complicated by the flagrant use of nicknames. One may find a person listed under his true surname in one place, and by a nickname in another. These names can sometimes be located when both names are given separated by the French verb "dit" or, if a woman, "dite." The translation of the word is "called," sometimes improperly noted as "alias." Seventeenth century French dictionaries relate the use of this word in the same way we speak of a nickname, and if one refers to the particular usage found in the census tables, one finds that this is more true than the attempt to hide one's baptismal surname under the guise of an alias.

Soldiers often used the name followed by a sobriquet or nickname specified to promote fear in the enemy, and we find numerous examples of one "called" Sansoucy, Sanschagrin, Sanfacon, meaning without care (free from care), without vexation (free from grief, apparently as related to the deed to be accomplished), and without ceremony, in that order.

Others use the verb "dit" to denote the place where they originated, for example - - - dit Langlois (- - - called Englishman), - - - dit Lionnois (- - - called the man from Lion). These sobriquets can often be used to determine where the particular person lived and even where his ancestors lived.

There are many other uses for the word "dit" between names, and this writer decided that the use was so thoroughly French that it would be improper to translate the word to "called" or "alias" as many reporters have done in the past.

The French words "beau," "bel" and "bon" which mean beautiful, handsome, becoming, and good, kind, favorable are descriptive adjectives which now form part of true surnames. These names often are nicknames but were carried as surnames by several generations before migrating to America. Sometimes they appear as "dit" names, where they can be traced to a particular quality of the bearer, but more often they are the property of the family as a true surname.

The reader is cautioned to survey names beginning with the letter "V" or the letters "Gu" as being possibly a French translation of a German surname beginning with the letter "W". Note for example, that the French name "Guillaume" is the German name "William." In the census records one will find also names such as "Vagneur," which is the German name "Wagner" and both "Vaguersbac" and "Wagensback" are found in different census tables for the same family.

For a more nearly complete study of French names, one is referred to the excellent work of Albert Dauzat, <u>Dictionnaire des Noms de Famille et Prenoms de France</u>, published by the Larousse firm in Paris.

In the census tables use has been made of the following abbreviations:

M. before a name signifies Monsieur. At the time of these census tables, this signified a person of dignity and position.

Made. signifies Madame, a position of dignity.

Mlle. signifies Mademoiselle, an unmarried woman of marriageable age.

Sieur or Le sieur was a title, almost a noble or aristocratic one. However, there were few Counts, Barons, or titled nobility in Louisiana. The title Sieur usually signifies a landowner or one having an almost aristocratic station.

Because of the complexity of name usage described above, the various factors should be kept in mind in searching for a name in the very extensive index at the back of this work. In addition, when a name is found, the whole page of text should be scanned, for the name sought may have been used more than once on that page.

CENSUS OF THE INHABITANTS OF THE
FIRST SETTLEMENT ON THE GULF COAST, FORT
MAUREPAS, DECEMBER 1699.

### OFFICERS:

M. de SAUVOLLE, commander, ensign, lieutenant
        of the company, from the vessel MARIN
M. de BIENVILLE de LONGUIL, lieutenant of the
        king, from the vessel BADINE
M. Le VASSEUR de BOUSSOUELLE, major, from the
        vessel BADINE, Canadian officer
M. de BORDENAVE, chaplan
PIERRE CAVE, surgeon major

### PETTY OFFICERS:

JEAN FRANCOIS Le VASSEUR, Master of a boat,
        from the vessel La PRECIEUSE
FRANCOIS GUYON, Master of a boat, from
        the vessel Le VOYAGEUR
NICOLAS La VOYE, Coastal Pilot, from the
        vessel BADINE
PIERRE TABATRAU, road pilot from LEOGANE
PHILIPES LEY, mastergunner, from the vessel
        BADINE

### SAILORS:

PIERRE HARDOUIN, ship carpenter, from the BADINE
RAYMOND SAINTOT, from the BADINE
BERNARD SAUROTTE, from the BADINE
JACQUES ROY dit GRIMOS, carpenter, from the
        vessel MARIN

### CANADIANS:

JACQUES BELLAIR
PIERRE POT
PHILIPES du COUDRET
PIERRE TESSERONTIE
ANTOINE DAMEDIEU
Le POLONNAIS
HURS Le ROY
CLAUDE MARANDAN
ESTIENNE GODEFRAY
JEAN Du CHESNE
ESTIENNE GODEFRAY
JEAN ERERY
JEAN PINTUREAU
JEAN du BOULLAY
JEAN BAPTISTE HERVIERS

A-99

JEAN CABUTEAU
TINEAU ALEXANDRE
LOUIS GUAY
ANTOINE OLIVER
      FREEBOOTERS:
PIERRE DESMAREZ
MICHEL CHESSE
NICOLAS de GARDE
JEAN NIMONNEAU
JEAN DESPLANES
PHILIPES PAGET
PIERRE BERTRAND
JACQUES EMERIT
ANDRE REGNAUX
JACQUES CAROLLE
JEAN CHARNEAUX
LOUIS Le DUC
PIERRE St. GERMAIN
      LABORERS:
JACQUES GOURDON, edge tool maker
FRANCOIS NICAUD, carpenter
ESTIENNE TARDIF
HENRY CROISY, cabinet maker using copper trusses
JEAN La PORTE, gunsmith
FRANCOIS de SALLE, shoemaker
ESTIENNE DUGUAY, baker
MARC ANTOINE BASSET
CLAUDE BAGE
PIERRE POTUS
      CABIN BOYS:
St. MICHEL
PIERRE HUET
GABRIEL MARCAL
JEAN JOLY
JACQUES CHARON
PIERRE Le VASSEUR
      SOLDIERS who remained at the fort:
DANIEL PINEAU dit La MOTTE, sergeant
FRANCOIS MONTIRON, corporal
JEAN DESGARENNES, corporal
PIERRE BOSSET
JACQUE PORCHE
HEYDEROME BROUIN
JEAN MALBEEG
JEAN MARPEAUX
PIERRE GODEAUX

                           A-99

GUILLAUME MARTIN
ANTOINE NIRET
JEAN CHESNE
JEAN du VAL
NICOLAS La TUILLE
JACQUES HENRY
PIERRE VALLET
PIERRE MAURY
MORGAN NOMME
PIERRE CILLIRAUX
GUILLAUME LUCAS

* * * * * * * * * *

CENSUS OF THE OFFICERS, PETTY OFFICERS,
SAILORS, CANADIANS, FREEBOOTERS, AND OTHERS
LOCATED AT BILOXI AS OF MAY 25, 1700

1. Staff Officers

    M. De SAUVOLIE, commandant
    M. de BIENVILLE, Lieutenant of the King
    M. de BOISBRIAND, Major
    M. Le VASSEUR, Canadian Officer
    M. de St. DENIS, Canadian Officer
    Father DuRUT, Jesuit Chaplain
    Le sieur CRASSE, Clerk for the King
    Le sieur CAVE, Surgeon Major

2. Petty Officers

    JEAN FRANCOIS Le VASSEUR, native of Quebec,
        Master of the ferry boat Le Precieuse
    NICOLAS La VOYE, native of La Rochelle,
        Coast Pilot
    PIERRE BERTRAND, native of Rochefort, Master
        Gunner
    JACQUES ROY, native of Havre de Grace,
        Carpenter
    JACQUES Le COMPTE, native of Rochefort,
        Master Caulker

3. Sailors

    PIERRE ARDOUIN, native of La Rochelle,
        Carpenter
    RAIMON SAINTOT, native of L'Isle de Re
    RAIMIN TRAIS, native of Bordeaux
    PIERRE FORCAN, native of La Marque
    LAURENT ROQUETTE, native of La Bastich
    LEONARD RICHARD
    ANDRE BOUCHERIE, native of Lormont
    MARTIN Le GUERAT, Native of Bayonne
    JEAN LAURENT, native of La Rochelle

4. Canadians

    JACQUES BELAIR
    PIERRE POT
    PHILIPPE COUDRAY
    PIERRE TESSERONTIERE
    RENE BOYER, Gunsmith of the ship La Renommee
        who replaced JEAN BAPTISTE HERVIEUX
    VINCENT ALEXANDRE
    ALEX FRANCOIS
    LOUIS GUAY

                          A-00

ANTOINE OLIVER
JOSEPH La POINTE
IGNACE La POINTE
FRANCOIS POUDRIEN
JOSEPH CHAUVIN
JEAN BAPTISTE GRAVELINE
JEAN LEVEILLE
CHARLES LAMOTTE
FRANCOIS MALTOT, who replaced JACQUEREAU
FRANCOIS La SOLAY
PIERRE TALON
ANDRE ROY
GILBERT d'ARDENNE
DENIS DURBOIS
ESTIENNE La CHAMBRE
JEAN BAPTISTE TURPIN
FRANCOIS CLAVERIE
CLEMENT BEGON
LOUIS LARRIVEE
MATHIEU BELLEFOND
PHILIPPE MINET
CHARLES Le VASSEUR
FRANCOIS BRETON
ANTOINE DAMEDIEU
IVES Le ROY
JEAN DUCHAINE
ESTIENNE GODEFROY
ANTOINE LUCAS
CLAUDE TREPANIER
CHARLES RENAUT
JOSEPH BOURBONNIERE
FRANCOIS MONTREUIL
FRANCOIS St. MARIE
JACQUES CHAUVIN
IGNACE LAVAL
PIERRE COUILLARD dit La FONTAINE
FRANCOIS HAMEL
PIERRE ALLAIN
CHARLES La ROZE
MARC BERICHON
NICOLAS LATOPINE
LOUIS BAUDCUIN
JEAN MIGNERON
JOSEPH ROBITAILLE
CLAUDE FRANCOEUR
SEBASTIAN CHARPENTIER

A-00

ANTOINE ROUSSAIN
JACQUES LABRY
LUC DOURINE
VILLEDIEU
FRANCOIS BONVALET
GUILLAUME St. TEREZE
JEAN LABARRE
5. Freebooters
MICHEL CHESSE
NICOLAS de SARDES
JEAN SIMONEAU
JEAN DESPLANS
PHILIPPE PAGET
PIERRE BERTRAND
JACQUES HEMERY
ANDRE RENAUD
LOUIS Le DUCQ
PIERRE St. GERMAIN
6. Laborers
FRANCOIS SICAUT, carpenter
JEAN LAPORTE, gunsmith
ESTIENNE TARDIT
CLAUDE BERGE
MARC ANTOINE BASSET
JEAN LUCAN, locksmith
7. Cabin boys
St. MICHEL
GABRIEL MARTIAL
JEAN JOLY
JACQUES CHARRON
FRANCOIS MOREAU
JACQUES DUPONT
8. Soldiers of the detachment of M. ROUSSEL
FRANCOIS CARRON dit LANGOUMOIS, sergeant
PIERRE LAURENDAU dit LANGOUMOIS, Corporal
JEAN HARUNE dit La ROCHE
9. Soldiers of the detachment of M. d'ARQUAIN
PIERRE BOJER dit BOUGUNDIAN
GEROME BROUAN dit La FOREST
PIERRE BEAUDEAU dit St. GEORGE
JEAN MARPEAU dit BEAUSEJOUR
La FONTAIN dit La ROZE
JEAN MALBECQ dit MALBECQ
ANTOINE SIRET
GUILLAUME MARTIN dit SANS CHAGRIN

A-00

10. Soldiers of the detachment of M. de BELICOURT
        PIERRE ROBERT dit La MONTAIGNE
        PIERRE MAURY dit DUCHAINE
        PIERRE TALLET dit POITEVIN
        NICOLAS LEGUAY dit SANS RAISON
11. Soldiers of the detachment of M. ROUSSEL
        JACQUES La COUR dit GRANDMAISON
        MAURICE CERGEAU dit La PLANTE
        PIERRE ROBERT dit CHAMPAIGNE
        FRANCOIS OLIVIER dit l'ESPERANCE
        JEAN BAPTISTE BONNEVIE dit FRANCOEUR

        *  *  *  *  *  *  *  *  *  *

LIST OF THE MARRIAGABLE GIRLS
WHO ARRIVED ABOARD THE PELICAN AT BILOXI
IN THE YEAR 1704

FRANCOISE MARIE AMME de BOISRENAUD
JEANNE CATHERINE de BERANHARD
JEANNE ELIZABETH Le PINTEUX
MARIE NOEL de MESNIL
GABRIELLE SAVARIT
GENEVIEVE BUREL
MARGUERITE BUREL
MARIE THERESE BROCHON
ANGELIQUE BROUPN
MARIE BRIARD
MARGUERITE TAVERNIER
ELIZABETH DESHAYS
CATHERINE CHRISTOPHLE
MARIE PHILIPPE
LOUISE MARGUERITE HOUSSEAU
MARIE MAGDELEINE PUANET
MARIE DuFRESNE
MARGUERITE GUICHARD
RENEE GILBERT
LOUISE FRANCOISE Le FEVRE
GABRIELLE BONET
MARIE JEAN MARBE
CATHERINE TOURNANT ( possibly did not come)

CENSUS OF THE HABITANTS OF FORT LOUIS
de la LOUISIANNE at MOBILE, TAKEN BY
NICOLAS de la SALLE, August 1, 1706

M. de la SALLE, wife, 4 children
GUILLAUME BOUTIN, wife
JEAN ROY, wife, 2 children
JEAN Le CAMP, who has the first child
     born in the colony
FRANCOIS MAY, wife, 2 children
NICOLAS La FRENIERE, a bachelor
FRANCOIS.TRUDEAU, wife, child
ESTIENNE BURELL, wife, child
widow La SUEUR, of Canada, with 3 girls
     and 1 boy
mademoiselle BOISRENAUD
GABRIELLE BONNET, woman, husband deserted
MICHEL RISKE
LAURENS CLOSTINY, child

     The following were in the pay
     of the king:
Le sieur BARRAU, wife
ANDRE RENAUD, wife, child
GILBERT DARDENNE, wife, child

\* \* \* \* \* \* \* \* \* \*

A-06

CENSUS OF FAMILIES AND HABITANTS OF
LOUISIANA TAKEN AUGUST 1, 1706
by NICOLAS de la SALLE

| | |
|---|---|
| M. de la SALLE, wife, 4 children | 6 persons |
| GUILLAUME BOUTIN, wife | 2 |
| JEAN ROY, wife, 2 children | 3 |
| JEAN La LOIRE, wife, child | 3 |
| JEAN Le CAMP, with the first child born in Louisiana | 2 |
| FRANCOIS MAY, wife, 2 children | 4 |
| NICOLAS LAFRENIERE, a boy | 1 |
| FRANCOIS. TRUDEAU, wife, child | 3 |
| ESTIENNE BURELLE wife, child | 3 |
| Madame widow Le SUEUR, of Canada, 3 girls, 1 boy | 5 |
| Mle. BOISRENAUD, girl | 1 |
| GABRIELLE BONNET, girl, her husband a deserter | 1 |
| MICHEL KISBE | 1 |
| LAURENSO CLOSTIGNY, child | 2 |

Those following are in the
pay of the king

| | |
|---|---|
| Le sieur BARRAU, wife | 2 |
| ANDRE RENAUD, wife, child | 3 |
| GILBERT DARDENNE, wife, child | 3 |
| PIERRE BRAVARD, wife, child | 3 |
| PIERRE ALLIN, wife, child | 3 |
| RENE BOYER, gunsmith, wife, child | 3 |
| JEAN BOURBONNOIS, wife, child | 3 |
| ANTOINE RIVARRI, wife, child | 3 |
| CLAUDE TREPANIER, wife, child | 3 |
| JEAN COULOMB, wife, 2 children | 4 |
| JOSEPH PENIGAUD, wife | 2 |
| JEAN SOSSIE, wife, 2 children | 4 |
| MARIE MERCIER, girl | 1 |
| MARIE CRESOT, midwife | 1 |
| MARIE LIGNAU, girl | 1 |
| JEAN LOUIS MINIUTY' wife, 2 children | 4 |
| ANNE PERRO, widow, 4 children | 5 |

total 85 persons

\* \* \* \* \* \* \* \* \* \*

CENSUS OF FORT LOUIS de la MOBILE
FROM THE MAP OF 1711

Streets running north to south parallel
to the river
1. Along the river, "front" street
POUARIE
La LOIRE
Le CONTE
jesuit fathers
La SALLE
d'YBERVILLE
2. Rue St. Francois
madame DIEU
L'ESPERANCE
La FONTAINE
GOULARD
JAQUE BOULLET
SENSGENS
TALLEMONT
BOUTIN
jesuit fathers
LAMERY
FRANCOUR
TREPAGNIER
CLAUDE
MINET
St. MARIE
Le SUEUR
Le VASSEUR
BOISBRILLANT
place royal
La LOIR
GERARD
SAVARIE
BOYER
Le MOINE
LOUIS Le DIEU
SABASTIEN
Le BRETON
ALEXANDRE
La FLEUR
L'ASSURE
3. Rue St. Joseph
BEAUSEJOUR
La CHENESGAULLE

A-11

CHARLE DUMONT
MARAIS
DUMONT, cadet
garden of the seminary
JEAN Le CAN
MAGDELEINE POULARD
JACQUE La POINTE
DENIS DURBOIS
CHAVIER (and his brother)
DOMINIQUE
FRANÇOIS MONTREUIL
AYOTE
de TONTI
CHARLEVILLE
PIERIE
La FOLETT
JACQUE La BARRE
LEZIE LARCOIS
ROUFFAIN
CHARLE REGNAULT
JEAN ALEXANDRE
BECCANCOUR
La FORCE
La FLEUR
DUHAUT MENI
JUCHERO
PIERRE IGOGUI
ANTOINE PRIAU
FRANÇOIS MARIE BOURNE
St. DENIS
St. MARIN
ALEXIE GRY
BIROTS
ANDRE PENEGAU
ROBILLARD
4. Rue Seminaire ( Seminary Street)
the cemetery
PIERRE Le SUEUR
ROY
de LAUNY
NEVEU
NEVEU the elder
La LIBERTE
DESLIST
NICOLAS LABERGE

A-11

```
                    FRANCOIS TRADO
                    Le BOEUF
                    La VALE
                    La SOURCE
                    MANUELLE du HAUTMENY
                    CHAUVIN the elder
                    LA FRENNIERE
5. Unnamed street on the west side
                    ROCHON
                    CHARLI
                    LEGAT
                    ANTOINE RINARD
                    MARTIN MOQUIR
                    ZACARE DRAPEAU
                    LANGLOIS
                          residents on the cross streets
                          not residing on the corners
6. Rue Charpentie
                    JEAN PARTIE
                    CONDITS
                    LOUIS DORE
7. Street of the Jesuits
                    Le VETIAS
                    REGNAULT
                    ALAIN
8. at the Place Royal
                    POUDRIE
9. Rue d'Yberville
                    JOSEPH La POINTE
                    DARDINE
                    FRANCOIS HAINELLE
                    BERICHON
                    Du ROCQUE
10. Rue Boisbrillant
                    Le GASCON
                    COURTOIS
                    Le NANTOIS
11. Rue Serigue
                    CHARLES MINET
                    PIERRE ARDOUIN
                    JEAN FRANCOIS LeVASSEUR
                    St. LAMBERT
                    De haut MENI
                    MICHEL PHILIPPE
```

2. Rue Bienville
       MATHIEU SAJAN
       JEAN SAUCIE

       Because of flooding the fort was moved in 1711
       to a point upriver. Maps for the new fort do
       not indicate habitants, however a few names
       appear in various documents:

       JEAN CHASTANG, mobile resident since 1704
       d'ARTAGUIETTE
       PAILLOU, aide major and engineer
       de VALIGNY
       BLONDEL, lieutenant
       La VIGNE VOISIN, captain from St. Malo
                  and resident of Dauphin Isle
       de CHATEAUGUE
       POIRRIER, commissary
       M. de St. HELEINE
       M. desLAUNIER , surgeon
       M. BLONDEL
       de BOISBRILLANT
       de GRANVILLE
       VALIGNY, a soldier
       St. DENIS
       JEAN LOUIS, a gunner
       DuCLOS, ordinance
       BIENVILLE
       de MANDEVILLE
       de PAILLOU, engineer
       ALEXANDRE. resident of dauphin isle
       La POINTE, carpenter from Longueil, Canada
       TRUDANT  carpenter from Longueuil, Canada
       LONGUEUIL, carpenter from Longueuil, Canada
       BENOIST, carpenter

              *  *  *  *  *  *  *  *  *  *

LIST OF OFFICERS COMMISSIONED AT FORT LOUIS
BILOXI, OCTOBER 25, 1713

Sieur de BIENVILLE, Commander
Sieur de BOISBRIANT, major
Sieur de VALIGNY, Adjutant major
Sieur de MALEFFRE, kings scribe, clerk of the
        council, commissary
Sieur POIRIER, warehouse guard at Ft. Louis
Sieur DHERBANNE, warehouse guard at Dauphin
        Island
Sieur ( name illegible) clerk at Ft. Louis
sieur DESLORIERS, surgeon major
sieur HUVE, chaplain

\* \* \* \* \* \* \* \* \* \*

PERSONS MENTIONED IN THE COLONY
BY ANTOINE de la MOTHE CADILLAC, October 1713

d'ARTAGUETTE
de REMONVILLE
de MANDEVILLE
PHILIPPE
La VIGNE ( said to be in Natchez)
Le sieur GRAVELINES
BIENVILLE,( Kings Lieutenant)
CHATEAUGUE, ( major)
BOISBRIANT,( said to be cousin to Bienville)
LANGLOIS, interpreter in Illinois, a canadian
        with wife
MAINVILLE, backwoodsman
ROY, of Detroit
St . MICHEL, discoverer of a silver mine
RICHARD, a discoverer of a silver mine
Le sieur de RICHEBOURG, a captain who arrived with
        Cadillac
VERDIER, ships stewart
BOUTIN
Le sieur POIRIER, warehouse guard
CARITON, said to be a deserter
BELLEC dit BOISVILLE
St. ANDRE dit COUTEVILLE
SAN FACON
La RIVIERE
CREPEAUX

A-13

## NOTES ON THE CENSUS OF 1721

The census of 1721 represents the remnants of the
large number of Frenchmen sent to the concessions
by the John Law enterprises. It is divided into
two parts by the census taker ( Le sieur Diron),
the first being the areas around New Orleans, then
only three years old, the second around the old
settlements of Mobile bay and Biloxi. This last
represents in addition to the newcomers, those who
remained from the original settlers of the Crozat
regime.

Totals of the census are in two parts, for the
New Orleans area, and for the Mobile area:

|  | New Orleans | Mobile | total |
|---|---|---|---|
| Frenchmen | 290 | 119 | |
| Frenchwomen | 140 | 95 | |
| French children | 96 | 113 | 853 |
| European engagees | 156 | 22 | |
| ( domestic servants) | | | 178 |
| Negro slaves | 533 | 247 | 680 |
| Indian slaves | 51 | 110 | 161 |

These are numbered in the following pages in the right
hand columns by masters, servants, negro slaves, and
indian slaves. No number in a column or a zero indicates
no one in that household of that classification.

The original of this census also shows the number of
cattle, and the number of horses.

The originals of these tables are signed by Diron, and
countersigned by Bienville and deLorme.

Although incomplete in themselves, the settled areas
missing from these census tables are in part continued
by the census of 1722 for the concessions along the
River St. Louis ( Mississippi) and the census for
Natchitoches, which along with the two tables for 1721
represents the French in the lower Mississippi valley
for this two year period.

Not included in these census tables are the soldiers
and military personnel in the area during the period.

GENERAL CENSUS OF ALL INHABITANTS OF
NEW ORLEANS AND ENVIRONS DATED NOVEMBER 24,
1721, AS REPORTED BY LE SIEUR DIRON.

1. New Orleans, inhabitants and concessionaires.
   M. de BIENVILLE, commander general

```
                                              2, 2,27, 7
   M. PAILHOUX, commandant                    1, 0, 8, 1
   Sieur BANES, major                         1, 2,
   De GAUVRY, captain, wife, child            3, 1, 5, 2
   De PAUGER, engineer                        1, 0, 2,
   DESCOUBLANS, officer                       1, 0, 1,
   De LATOUR, officer                         1, 0, 1,
   BASSET, officer                            1, 0, 1,
   COUSTILLAS, officer                        1, 3,12,
   DUPUY, officer, wife, child                3, 0, 5,
   ROSSARD, notary and attorney               1, 0, 1,
   BERARD, surgeon major                      1, 0, 1, 2
   BERARD the younger, wife                   2, 1,
   TRUDEAU, wife, 7 children                  9, 2,31, 1
   SARAZIN, warehouse guard, wife             2, 0, 2, 1
   BRULE, wife, 3 children                    5, 0, 3, 1
   EDME LUCIEN PORRE, gunsmith, wife          2, 0, 1,
   BONNEAU, captain of the company's
             ship, wife                       2,
   PIERRE and MATHURIN DREUX,
             brothers                         2,10, 8, 2
   BELLEGARDE, baker                          1,
   MATHURIN ROY, gunsmith                     1, 0, 1,
   HENRI BRIGNOIS, joiner, wife               2, 0, 3,
   The widow DUGENOIS                         1,
   JEAN REYMOND, wife, child                  3,
   JACQUES KIVEZ, retired sergeant,
             wife                             2, 0, 6,
   PIERRE AUBERT, locksmith, wife,
             child                            3, 1, 2,
   LOUIS de LASSUS                            1, 0, 1,
   GERMAIN BERTIN, shoemaker,
             wife, child                      3, 0, 1,
   PIERRE DEMUN, tailor, wife                 2,
   MICHEL de CUVES, carpenter,
             ex- soldier, wife                2, 1, 2,
   JACQUES LEMAIRE, butcher                   1,
   VEILLON, turner                            1,
```

```
RIFFAUD, house dresser                 1,
the wife of BELAIR, soldier,
          2 children                   3, 0, 1,
CARITON, tailor, wife                  2, 0, 1,
the wife of LEBRETON                   1,
TURPIN, wool (comber?) canadian        1, 0, 2, 2
VILLEUR                                1,
ROY, canadian, wife                    2, 0, 2,
La VIOLETTE, wife                      2, 0, 1,
RICHAUME, canadian, wife               2, 0, 2,
the wife of La RIVIERE                 1,
TOMELIN, joiner, 3 children            4,
PIERRE ANTOINE DUFLAU, wife,
          child                        3,
BERTRAND JAFFRE, wife                  2, 0, 3,
HEBERT and PROVINCHE, associates       2, 0, 5,
VIGER                                  1, 0, 7,
DULUTH                                 1, 0, 2,
BIGOT                                  1, 0, 0, 1
widow of one called SANS SOUCY,
          child                        2,
JEAN COFFINE, maker of tobacco,
          wife, child                  3,
JEAN FREDERIC FREITAG, wife,
          child                        3,
LOUIS ESTIENNE, engraver, wife         2,
Le BLANC, warehouse guard,
          storekeeper                  1, 3, 6, 1
JOLY, joiner                           1,
ADRIAN FLAMANT, gardner, wife,
          child                        3,
BONNAUD, secretary to M. Diron,
          wife, child                  3, 0, 6,
TRAVERS, Tailor                        1, 1, 1,
GODET                                  1, 0, 1,
BLANCHY, wife                          2, 0, 1,
BARROY                                 1, 0, 2,
LEMPILEUR                              1, 0, 1,
L'ABBE. pastry cook, wife, child       3, 0, 1
the widow of BOUCHARD, officer         1,
```

2. New Orleans, persons in the service of the company.

```
CAYEUX dit St. GERMAIN                 1,
PIERRE PINAU, carpenter                1,
PEREAU, carpenter                      1,
BUREAU, carpenter                      1,
JACQUES ROCHARD, carpenter, wife       2,
                                       A-21
```

```
JULIEN BINARD dit La FORGE,
          blacksmith, wife           2,
PIERRE FOUCHE , ships master         1,
PIERRE BEL, caulker                  1,
JEAN VANGUEN, caulker, wife          2,
GUILLAUME Le FRANCOIS, waggoner      1,
FRANCOIS FIOU, overseer, wife        2,
De BRYE                              1,
PASCAL, ship master, wife,
          2 children                 4, 1,
J- FRANCE, ships master, wife,
          child                      3, 0, 1,
La BORDE, ships master, wife         2,
MERIE dit SANS CHAGRIN, ships
          master, wife               2,
La MESSE, wife, child                3,
MAZELIERE, ships master              1,
FRANCOIS GUERNAZIOU, ships master    1,
PIERRE ROBERT, joiner                1,
PIERRE MOREL, joiner                 1,
JEAN ROBERT, locksmith               1,
VALLE, commander of the negroes      1,
HORZE, edge tool maker, wife         2,
L: FRESNE, ships master              1,
MARCHAND, ships master, wife         2,
MAIGRE, ships master                 1,
MAGON, ships master                  1,
MASSIERE, ships master, wife,
          2 children                 4,
Le NANTOIS, ships master, wife,
          child                      3,
Du ROCHER, ships master              1,
BLANCHARD, ships master              1,
VACHON, ships master                 1,
FRANCOIS CHERO, ships master         1,
DIONGUE, ships master, wife, child   3,
The wife of one named MARMANDE,
          3 children                 4,
woman named FRANCOISE LABROSSE       1,
JULLIEN MOUSSET, sailor              1,
CLAUDE Le CLAIR, sailor              1,
GILLES HORY, sailor                  1,
CAYON, sailor                        1,
FRANCOIS GUILLOIN, sailor            1,
La PIERRE, sailor                    1,
```

A-21

```
                The daughter of St. MICHEL      1,
            GENDREAU, sailor                    1,
            FRANCOIS BOULEAU, sailor            1,
            Le VANEUR, sailor                   1,
            VILLEUR                             1,
3. New Orleans, forced immigrants (men)
            ANTOINE CAMUS                       1,
            JACQUES GUILLAUME                   1,
            LOUIS RIBERT                        1,
            LAVIGNE                             1,
            THOMAS FOISSARD                     1,
            L'EPINIERE                          1,
            PIERRE MARY                         1,
            BONVOISIN                           1,
            TOUREZ                              1,
            JOSEPH LEGER                        1,
            CAPET                               1,
            DURIVEAU                            1,
            FRANCOIS La CLEF                     1,
            PARABON                             1,
            NICOLAS QUGU                        1,
            NICOLAS MOUTEL                      1,
            BIDAUD                              1,
            NICOLAS SYZEAUX                     1,
            ANDRE Le NOIR                       1,
            CRISTOPHLE                          1,
            DUPRE                               1,
            CHARLES TEXIER                      1,
            VINCENT Le GOF                      1,
            LOUIS MENAGER                       1,
            RENAUDAN                            1,
            ANTOINE MORON                       1,
            LOUIS BASSE                         1,
            PIERRON                             1,
            IZAAC PELLE                         1,
            THOMAS DESMARRES                    1,
            La VIOLETTE                         1,
            CLERMONT                            1,
            JEAN VILLARD                        1,
            FRANCOIS CORSEY                     1,
            La ROQUETTE                         1,
            La TERREUR                          1,
            BOURBONNOIS                         1,
            BOURGUIGNON                         1,
            La FRANCE                           1,
```

```
          LOUIS BELLANOUE                        1,
          GUILLAUME CASTANOUE                    1,
          MARS Le GOF                            1,
4. New Orleans, forced immigrants (women)
          JOLLY                                  1,
          BLANCHE                                1,
          The wife of La VIOLETTE                1,
          The mother of  CRISTOPHLE              1,
          MARGUERITE  TELLIER                    1,
          JEANNE Le TRILLARD                     1,
          ANNE NAMONT                            1,
          LENOS                                  1,
          MAGDELAINE POUTON                      1,
          woman named RICHARD FRONTEVEAU         1,
          MARIE BOYER                            1,
          LOUISE FONTENELLE                      1,
          SUZANNE HYVER                          1,
5. The village on the Bayou St. John
          RIVARD or La VIGNE, wife,
                  6 children               8, 0,11, 2
          FRANCOIS DUGUE                   1, 0, 3, 3
          LANGLOIS, wife, child           3, 0, 8, 1
          JOSEPH GIRARDY, wife, 2 children  4, 0,10, 2
6. Old village of the Colapissa Indians
          M. de BEAUNE, former procurer
                  general, wife,
                  2 children              4, 3, 9,
7. The village called Chapitoulas
          Le sieur Du BREUIL, wife,
                  2 children              4, 2,43, 2
          LANTHEAUME,                     1, 1, 1,
          De LERY, 3 children             4, 1,33, 4
          La FRENIERE                     1, 5,53, 8
          BEAULIEU                        1, 0,30, 1
          JEAN TRONION and PIERRE DOUBLET,
                  Associates              2, 0, 1,
          Concession of M. COLLY ( Kolly)
                  (62 Frenchmen, 12 frenchwomen,
                  5 children, 46 negroes,
                  2 indians)             79, 0,46, 2
          DARCOURT ( Dalcourt?), wife      2, 2,11,
          MASSY                           1, 5, 8,
          Concession of M. Le BLANC
                  ( 7 frenchmen, 1 french-
                  woman)                  8,
```

8. The village called Gentilly
        SAINTON, wife, child           3, 3, 5, 1
        VIELLE VILLE, wife, child     3, 0, 1,
        La VIGNE, wife, child         3, 1,
        LANGEVIN                    1, 0, 3,
9. The village of Cannes Bruslee
        M. DIRON, Inspector General of the
                Troops of Louisiana,
                (1 frenchman, 6 frenchwomen,
                1 child, 20 french domestics,
                20 negroes, 2 indians)  8,20,20, 2
        Concession of M. Le Conte
        d'ARTAGNAN, (47 frenchmen, 8 french-
                women, 3 children,
                20 negroes)         58, 0,20,
        Le sieur St. JULIEN, former
                officer             1, 3, 8, 1
10. The place called Le Petit Dezert
        Concession of M. Le BLANC,
                (1 frenchman, 5 frenchwomen,
                7 french domestics,
                9 negroes)          6, 7, 9,
11. The place called English Turn ( Detour des Anglois)
    or Chaouchas.
        Concession of M. DUMANOIR
                (3 frenchwomen, 6 french
                domestics)         3, 6,
        Concession of M. Le BLANC
                (3 frenchmen, 20 frenchwomen,
                16 children, 28 french
                domestics, 2 negroes) 39,28, 2,
        Concession of M. LAW
                ( 5 frenchmen, 11 frenchwomen,
                14 children, 40 french
                domestics)         40,40,
        Le sieur DESLAU           1, 0, 6, 1

\* \* \* \* \* \* \* \* \* \*

CENSUS OF INHABITANTS IN THE AREA
OF BILOXI AND MOBILE, DATED JUNE 26, 1721,
AS REPORTED BY LE SIEUR DIRON

1. Habitants of Fort Louis de la Mobile

| | |
|---|---|
| M. de BIENVILLE | 1, 1, 6, |
| M. de CHATEAUGUE, lieutant of the King | 1, 1, 5, 3 |
| M. de LATOUR, Commandant, wife | 2, 5,14, 4 |
| M. de RICHEBOURG, Captain | 1, 1, 1, |
| JEAN ROY, gunner, 5 children | 6, 0, 8, 1 |
| Le sieur SARRAZIN, warehouse guard, wife | 2, 0, 2, 3 |
| JACQUES Le COMTE, caulker, wife | 2, 0, 3, 2 |
| PIERRE ALLAIN, blacksmith, wife, 3 children | 5, 0, 5, 1 |
| Le sieur DUCHE, Interpreter, wife, 2 children | 4, |
| FRANCOIS DUPRE, carpenter, wife, 5 children | 7, |
| NICOLAS MEUSNIER, wife, child | 3, 0, 1, |
| JEAN COUTURIER, child | 2, 0, 2, |
| ROSE URSULLE LIMOUNIERE ( madam) | 1, |
| M. BAJOT, former captain | 1, 0, 3, |
| LOUIS BREST, tailor, 5 children | 6, |
| LOUIS BOURBON, wife | 2, |
| RENE BOISSINOT de LAUZE, wife, 4 children | 6, 2, 0, 2 |
| ROBERT TALLOIN, joiner, wife | 2, 0, 5, 1 |
| JACQUE PINAU, baker, wife, 2 children, and PIERRE PHILIPES, associate | 5, |
| ESTIENNE MARTIN and FRANCOIS GUILLOT, associates | 3, |
| JEAN MESNAU dit BEAULIEU | 2, |
| Madam BOISARNAUD | 1, 0, 1, |
| JEAN BON, gunsmith, wife | 2, |
| ESTIENNE FIOU and JACQUES DuBOIS, Carpenter associates with one woman | 3, 0, 5, 1 |
| PIERRE PAQUET, tailor, wife, 2 children | 4, 1, 0, 2 |
| JEAN CHERANT, joiner, wife | 2, |
| JACQUES SAUNIER, edge tool maker, wife | 2, |

```
JEAN BEAURAY, edge tool maker,
          wife                        2,
ANTOINNE MICAUD, carpenter, wife   2, 0, 1,
Madam MARIE Le MAIRE                  1,
GABRIEL PRENAN dit La CHAUME,
          wife                        2,
Madam ANGELIQUE REFFE                 1,
DENIS JACOTEAU                        1,
NICOLAS LANEAU                        1,
ELIZABETH BERNARD, Madam              1,
M. GUERIN, officer, wife           2, 0, 1,
ANTOINNE PREREAU, goldsmith, wife,
          child                      3,
JEANNE VERGUE, and her child         2,
Le sieur RAGUET, Notary, wife      2, 0,10, 8
M. De LUCER, Officer, wife,
          3 children               5, 0, 1, 2
ESTIENNE BUREL, wife               2, 0, 2,
JOSEPH CARRIERE                    1, 0, 7, 2
Le sieur MANADE, surgeon major,
          wife                     2, 0, 3,37
Le sieur JOUSSET La LOIRE             1,
FRANCOIS CARRIERE, wife,
          2 children               4, 0,18, 7
Le sieur Des BROSSES, Warehouse Guard,
          wife                     2, 0, 1,
FRANCOIS ALLEVIN, gunsmith         1, 0, 1, 1
SAVIGNAN BRETON, wife, 2 children  4, 1,
BALTAZAR BARTHELEMY, wife,
          4 children               6, 0, 0, 1
St. AGNAN, wife                    2, 2,
woman named MARGUERITE             1, 0, 1,
La SONDE, surgeon                  1, 0, 1,
MATHIER ROGER, shoemaker,
          wife, child                3,
IZAAC DEDIE, wife, 2 children        3,
PIERRE Le GARD, locksmith,
          wife, 2 children         4, 1,
Madam Le SUEUR, 2 children         3, 0, 4, 1
MARGARITE CHEVALIER, wife of a
          soldier                    1,
MARIANNE FOUCHER, wife of a
          soldier                    1,
FRANCOIS DEVEAUX, wife of a
          soldier                    1,
```

```
ANNE THIBAUD, wife of a soldier,
          child                       2,
MARIE MARGUERITE RAX, wife of a
          soldier                     1,
MAGDELAINE FONTAINE, wife of a
          soldier                     1,
CATHERINE CHASSEAU, wife of a
          soldier                     1,
MAGDELAINE BEAUDOUIN, wife of a
          soldier                     1,
MARIE SARRAZIN, wife of a coldier 1,
JEANNE FONTAINE, wife of a soldier1,
BARBE CONRAD, wife of a soldier,
          child                       2,
MARGUERITE BAUDOUIN, wife of a
          soldier                     1,
RENE MARTIN, wife                     2,
JACQUES SALLEAU,    overseer,
          wife, child                 3,
MARIANNE BROSSARD, madam              1,
JEAN MALAU, blacksmith, wife          2,
JEANNE PONILLOT, wife of a
          soldier                     1,
MARIE TACHENAY, wife of a soldier 1,
MARIE BOUYE, wife of a soldier    1,
JEAN NOLLAND, irishman            1, 0, 5,
CHARLETTE VANHIR, wife of a
          soldier                     1,
DOMINIGUE BELSAGUI, pine tar
          maker, wife, 2 children 4, 1,15, 4
JEANNE VALLON, wife of a soldier  1,
RENE BOYER, PIERRE METAY, JEAN
          BEDUIREAU, RENE LAME,
          associates                  4,
Le sieur Du BREUIL, wife, 4
          4 children              6, 0, 5, 2
ANDRE CARRIERE, wife, child       3, 1,18, 6
RENE BESON, tanner, wife,
          2 children                  4,
PIERRE ROCHON, wife, 2 children   4, 0,10, 6
```

2. The village of the Apalaches ( called St. Louis)

```
PIERRE DRILLANT, wife, child      3, 0, 0, 5
LOUIS De FLANDRE, wife            2, 1,
PIERRE DESORDES, wife, child with
          ANTOINE FOURNEUR, wife
          child, associates          6
```

```
              Le sieur TREPANIER, wife,
                      7 children              9, 0,16, 3
              JEAN SANSON, wife, 4 children   6, 0, 4, 1
              JEAN Le MAIRE, wife             2,
              JEAN BAPTISTE BARRE, wife       2,
              JEAN La LOURE, wife, child      3, 0, 3, 4
              JULLIEN                         1,
              LOUIS BUREL                     1, 0, 9, 4
3. The village of the Mobiliens ( Called l'Ecor St.
      Herme)
              ALEXANDRE La LANDE, Irishman,
                      wife, 2 children        4, 0, 1
4. Village of the Fourches
              DONNEIL                         1, 1,
              CHAMPIGIN                       1,
              JEAN VALLADE dit DRAPEAU, wife,
                      2 children              6, 5, 3,
              GILLEBERT JARDENNE, child       2, 0, 2, 1
              CLAUDE PARANT, wife, child, with
                      RENE ANDRIEN dit
                      POUCHATEAU, associates  4, 1,10, 5
5. Village of the Tomes
              JEAN VALANTIN CANEL, wife, child  3, 0, 5,
              FRANCOIS CANEL                  1,
              JEAN COLOMB dit La VIOLETTE,
                      wife, 6 children        8, 0, 6, 1
              La CARIE DRAPEAU, carpenter,
                      wife, 2 children        4, 0, 2, 5
              RENE CHESNE with ANDRE PEAU, his
                      wife, 2 children        4, 0, 2, 5
6. Village of the Muniaba
              JEAN VEUILLE, wife, child       3, 0, 4,
              ANDRE POITEVIN and THOMAS FLEURY,
                      associates              2,
7. Village of the Apalaches,(called Petit Ecor)
              CHARLES VAUTIER                 1, 1
              PIERRE La VIGNE, wife           2,
              PIERRE DESANDRE dit LANDRECY,
                      wife                    2,
              JEAN LAURENCON dit BEAUDIEU,
                      wife                    2,
              PIERRE VAUTIER, wife            2,
8. Village of the Taensas
              JOSEPH BUREAU                   1,
              LOUIS d'AUTERIVE                1,
              JEAN BAPTISTE BRAQUET           1,
                                              B-21
```

```
 9. Habitants of d'Ille Dauphine
        Le sieur ARNAUD                        1, 0, 5, 5
        GUILLAUME HUET, wife, 4 children       6, 0, 2, 3
        PIERRE HUBERT dit DUPLESSIS,
                wife, 2 children               4,
        JEAN BARRAUD, child                    2,
        MICHEL DANTY dit LAUVERGNE,
                wife, child                    3,
        widow ALLEXANDRE, 4 children           5,
        LEVESQUE, wife, 5 children             7,
10. Habitants with the Alibamons
        MICHEL BOURICHON,
        JEAN BRUTEL,
        FRANCOIS VILLELEGER, associates        3,
        NICOLAS LOCART,
        JULLIEN FIGAUD, associates             2,
        VINCENT AMIET,
        FRANCOIS CHEVRIER,
        JACQUES SAVETIER, associates           3,
        SIMON BRAQUA,
        LAURENT LAURENT, associates            2,
        LOUIS AUTIAUMY,
        PIERRE GUIGON, associates              2,
        MICHEL GUARIN                          1,
            *  *  *  *  *  *  *  *  *  *
```

CENSUS OF HABITANTS OF THE CONCESSIONS
ALONG THE MISSISSIPPI RIVER DATED MAY 13, 1722
AS REPORTED BY SIEUR DIRON

1. In the place called Allemands, there are 3 men,
        3 women, 7 children.
2. In the place called St. Reyne there are 12 men,
        1 woman, 1 child.
3. MATHIEU DUFLOS, and his associate
        CLAUDE RIVIERE
4. SAINTON, wife, 1 child.
5. Le Sieur DELAIR, Concessionaire, another man, wife.
6. Village of Catslings ( Portefax?), habitant
        Le Sieur d'ARINSBOURG, Captain
7. Village of Mariedal, with 25 men, 30 women, 25 child-
        ren.
8. Village of Wess, with 25 men, 29 women, 40 infants
9. Village of Ausberg, with 17 men, 20 women, 33 child-
        ren.
10. Village of Grande Colas, habitants:
        BESSON, wife
        BISCORNET, wife
11. Village of Petit Colas, habitants:
        le sieur de CHAVANNE, with 3 other men,
        4 women.
12. Village of Petit Hommes ( Little Men), habitants:
        FRANCOIS COTTIN
        FRANCOIS CHEVAL, wife, child
        JEAN BORDIER, wife, child
        FRANCOIS Le COMTE, wife
        ANTHOINE PINEAU, wife.
13. Village of Grande Hommes ( Big Men), habitants:
        PIERRE DROCOURT, with another man
        PIERRE BARROZ, wife
        ESTIENNE CHAIGNEAU, 3 children
        LOUIS ROUSSEAU dit La FLAME, wife
        widow La CROIX, child.
14. Ancient village of Chitmacha , Habitants:
        Le sieur DUBUISSON, with 8 men, 3 women,
        2 children
        St. MARTIN, wife.
15. BATON ROUGE, Concession of DIRON, Habitants:
        ten men, 5 women, 2 children

16. Concession called Terre Blanche, Habitants:
      Le Sieur de MEZIERES, with 13 men, 6 women.
17. Concession called St. Reyne, located at Pointe Coupee,
               with 15 men, 5 women, 2 children.
18. Indian village called Thominea, Habitants:
        JACQUES ROMAND
        JEAN RONDEAU, wife
        THOMAS ASSELIN, wife
        FRANCOIS NICOLAS de KUNPER, another man, wife,
                  one child
        LOUIS GOUZET, wife
        THOMAS RAYMONT, wife
        ANDRE GEORGE, with one named FRANCOIS, woman.
        JEAN CHARON
        BONHOME, with one named FRANCOIS
19. Census of Natchez, concessions of Le Blanc, Kolly
               (Coly)and Company, Concession of
               St. Catherine.
      St.Catherine consist of 43 men, 8 women,
           2 children.
      Concession of Le Blanc consist of 15 men,
           2 women
      Concession of Coly consist of 15 men, 5 women,
           5 children.
      The habitants include the following:
      GEDEMFREMY, wife, 2 children
      DUFOUR, wife, 2 children
      VILLENEUVE
      MONTUIS, wife
      PAJOIN, wife
      BEAUSOLEIL
      DUBIGNON
      BOURDON, wife, child
      HENRY
      GOULAIN, wife, 2 children
      COUTURIER
      FLANDRIN, wife
      La VIOLETTE, wife
      ROUISSON, wife
      JEAN BARSIN, wife
      LALANDE
      VERNAY, wife
      QUIAS
      GOUPIL
      PAUCHEUX
      HENRY VERLOIN

MICHEL ROGER et FRANCOIS FROTIN, and associates
ANDRE GEORGES, wife
CLAUDE SOLEIL
GABRIEL MACIOT et LOUIS TOUET, and associates
PELERIN & CACHE, associates
Le PAGE
BONAVENTURE
BLOUET
ZORANEO ( or QURANEO)
LOUIS ROUSSEAU, wife.
La SONDE, surgeon
Du MENY, wife
MICHEL Du BIGNON, wife
NOEL SOLAU, wife
CHARENTE, wife
BOUCHIN, wife
Le BLONDIN, wife
BACHERE
MOUTU et BOULOGNE, and associates
ROUSSEAU et La COMBE, and associates, with one
        woman.
FRANCISQUE
La LOIRE et MALO, company commissary
BELIOUR, wife.
20. Census of habitants established to work on the
                concession of Mr Law on the
                Acansaw ( Arkansaw), consisting of
                14 men, 1 woman, habitants
                including the following:
JACQUES CANTRELLE, wife
LOUIS HOMMIER, wife
PIERRE d'OVIDEAU et DOMINIQUE DARABI, associates
        with one woman
LORANS CONTANSO, wife
JAN BACHEL et GOUGINARI, associates
JACQUES d'ARCLON
JEAN CODE et BLOUIN DUGUE, associates
JACQUES MICHEL et RENAUT BARTHELEMY, associates,
        with one woman
MICHEL Le MOINE et ALLERIS CONARD, associates,
        with one woman
JEAN BOURGAIS
ANTHOINE GABIGNON

\* \* \* \* \* \* \* \* \* \*

CENSUS OF THE HABITANTS OF NAUCHITOCHES,
FORT St. JEAN BAPTISTE TAKEN FOR SIEUR
DIRON, GENERAL OF THE TROOPS, May 1, 1722

M. de St. DENIS, commandant
        2 children,5 negro slaves,
        4 indian slaves
Le sieur REDOT, lieutenant of the
        company ( on his land),
        1 indian slave
Le sieur DUPUY, ensign, (on his
        land) 4 negro slaves
Le sieur CLAUSSON, retired lieutenant,
        with one domestic
Le sieur DERBANNE, warehouse guard,
        3 children,4 negro slaves,
        3 indian slaves
Le sieur JALLOT
PIERRE COTOLLEAU
PIERRE FAUSSE
INES LION
FRANCOIS BERRY
FRANCOIS LEMOINE, wife
ESTIENNE LEROY
PIERRE DUBOIS
MARIANNE BENOIST, wife of a soldier
LOUISE FRANCOISE ZILLOT, wife of a soldier
JEANNE LONGUEVILLE, wife of a soldier
PIERRE DUPUY dit GOUPILLON, wife
JEANNE GRENOT, wife of a soldier
MARIE CATHERINE de POUTRE, wife of a soldier
MARTINE BONNET, wife of a soldier, child
ANTOINETTE AUDEBRAUD, wife of a soldier
PIERRE MARIONNEAU, 3 negro slaves
widow of PIERRIER, 4 children,3 negro
                slaves
Le sieur de CHAMPIGNOLE, sergeant,
        (on his land) 1 negro slave

Total 14 men, 10 women, 10 children,
      20 negro slaves, 8 indian slaves

\* \* \* \* \* \* \* \* \* \*

OFFICIALS OF THE COLONY OF LOUISIANA
APPOINTED AT FORT LOUIS, BILOXI, 1722

1. The superior council for Louisiana
        M.de BIENVILLE
        M. dela TOUR
        M.de CHATEAUGUE
        M.de LORMES
        M. BION
2. In charge of the records of the hospital
        M. dela GERARDIERE
        Chevalier de LOUBOEY
3. Civilian officials of the company
        Le sieur MICHEL, clerk
        Le sieur de VAUZE, bookkeeper ( discharged )
        Le sieur MALAFAIRE, clerk
        St. MICHEL, clerk
        BION, clerk, official head clerk
        Le sieur St. QUENTIN, scribe
        Le sieur TIXERAND, warehouse guard
        Le sieur LANGLOIS, warehouse bookkeeper
        Le sieur DUTOUR, assistant warehouse bookkeeper
        Sieur ESTIENNE, keeper of provisions
        Sieur La SALLE, assistant keeper of provisions
        Sieur DALCOURT, cashier
        Sieur La GOUBLAY, clerk to the cashier
        Sieur RAGUET, clerk to the council
4. Officials at Ship Island
        Le sieur VALLETTE, warehouse guard
        Le sieur GOUINT, assistant warehouse guard
5. Officials at New Orleans
        Le sieur MARLOT, chief clerk
        Le sieur DRILLAND, warehouse guard
        ( blank) apprentice clerk
        Le sieur Le BLANC, keeper of provisions
        Le sieur ROSSARD, notary and clerk
6. Officials at Natchez
        Le sieur de la LOERE  chief clerk, warehouse guard
        Le sieur La BRAU, inspector of tobacco
7. Officials at Natchitoches
        Le sieur DERBANNE, chief clerk and warehouse
                guard
8, Officials at Illinois
        Le sieur dela LOIRE des URSINS, chief clerk
                and warehouse guard
        Le sieur CHASSIN, assistant warehouse guard
                                                C-22

                 Le sieur PERILLAUD, warehouse clerk
 9. Officials at Missouri
                 (blank) clerk and warehouse guard
10. Officials at Arkansas
                 Le sieur Le HOUX, clerk and warehouse guard
11. Officials at Mobile
                 Le sieur DURAND, chief clerk and bookeeper
                 Le sieur VRAND, assistant warehouse guard
                 (blank) apprentice clerk
12. Officials at Alabamas
                 Le sieur La LANDE, clerk and warehouse guard
13. Additional officials:
                 BEAULIEU, appointed to sell beverages,
                          he is also corporal of the garrison
                 DANVILLE, keeper of a shop for merchandise
                          or provisions
                 CHASSIN, officer at the Illinois post
                 BOBE, missionary at Illinois
                 MELIQUE, concession owner at Illinois
                 RENAULT, assayer, miner at Illinois
                 SHAUMUR, officer at Illinois
                 Le BLANC, concessionaire

SOME COLONIST OF LOUISIANA MENTIONED
IN A LETTER BY DELACHAISE DATED APRIL 8, 1723


De la CHAISE, governor of the colony
replacing de LORME
Le sieur DESMOULINS, captain of the ship
        Galatee
Le sieur BONNEFOY, clerk of the vessel Galatee
Le sieur De VAUBERCY, ensign on the vessel
        Galatee
Le sieur de LOUBOEY, Commandant of Ft. Louis,
        Biloxi
Le sieur de LORME
CHEVALIER, owner of a small boat
PERRY, woman with 2 children aboard the
        Galatee
CORDE, a boatman in Biloxi
CHAVILIE, engineer
DILON, captain
NOYAN, ensign
Le sieur Le BLANC, captain
M. de BIENVILLE
M. de la TOUR
VALADON
ESTIENNE, acting clerk replacing BOURGES
Le sieur DALCOURT, former cashier
Le sieur CHESNEAU, Captain of the vessel
        La Loire
M. Du SAUNOY who died April 7, 1724
FAZENDE
Le sieur ALEXANDRE, surgeon at Chaouachas
Le sieur MALADET, surgeon
Le sieur BRULE
M. PERRY
FLEURIEU
BONNEAUD, warehouse guard
Le sieur SARAZIN, warehouse guard at Mobile
Le sieur DURAND, warehouse guard at Mobile
St. MARTIN, head bookkeeper
Le sieur de VAUZE, bookkeeper now recalled
GAILLET
BION
HUBERT
Le sieur PETIT, former secretary to Bienville

                                    A-23

M. de BOISPINEL, engineer
DIRON, inspector
Le sieur COLLARD, swiss officer
Le sieur BARON
BOUQUES, who died in the summer of 1724
JOYEUSE, surgeon
   POUILLADON de la TOUR, surgeon
who arrived August 8, 1722
AMELOT
woman named Le SUEUR, a relative of Bienville
   on Dauphin Island
JOLYBOIS
de LUSSER and wife
PAILLOUX, adjuctant general
Le sieur BANNES, adjuctant
Le sieur DUPUY, assistant adjuctant
DUTERPUY, adjuctant at Biloxi
Le sieur de la SALLE, at Mobile
Le sieur de MANDEVILLE
M. de CHATEAUGUE at Mobile
RENAULT, operating a lead mine in Illinois
Le sieur MASSY, operating an Indigo plantation
Le sieur BELAIR, lieutenant who died
ARNAUD, surgeon
Count d'ARQUIN, surgeon major
Le sieur de FLANDRE who arrived on the Galatee
Le sieur LONGVERT
THIERRY
Du RIVAGE, a ship builder, contractor, and
    appraiser
Le sieur MASCLARY of Mobile
Le sieur La PERRIERE, of Mobile
DESBROSSES
DUVAL, auditor for the company
CLAIRAC
Le BLANC, concessionaire
de BERNEVAL, commandant at Natchez
Le sieur La BRO, clerk
Le sieur MONPLAISIR, clerk
Le sieur AMERVAL, ensign at Mobile
Le sieur de VIEUGE, former ensign
Le sieur deMONTMONT, captain
TIXERANT, former warehouse guard at Mobile
Le sieur de GRAVES, Captain at Natchez
Le sieur DUMONT de MONTIGNY, second lieutenant
    of the Le Blanc concession at Natchez

Le sieur DUPUY PLANCHARD, adjutant major
Du ROUVROY
De L'AIRE
ROSSARD
RAGUET
Le sieur MARLOT, former warehouse guard at
        Mobile ( in 1718)
Le sieur La LOIRE.at Natchez
Le sieur DUMANOIR
Le sieur DUBREUIL at Mobile
Le sieur PELLERIN
St. JULIEN
de RICHEBOURG returned to France
Le sieur CHARTIER de BAULNE, Attorney General
LAZOU, captain of a small vessel
Le sieur DUCHESNE, concession of Kolly
De PAUGER
ADRIEN GILBERT of St. Malo
BOURBAUD, supplier of timber
SURATTE, a sailor
Father ANTOINE DAVION, missionary
        at Tunica
Father MONTIGNY, missionary
Father St. COSME, missionary in 1704
de CHAVANNES
Le sieur POCHOT, clerk for Dela Chaise
BLANCHARD, son of a lawyer of Paris
PHILIPPE RENAULT, banker turned miner
DURAND, clerk in Mobile
DUVAL, clerk in Mobile
CHASSIN, clerk in Mobile
Le sieur MASSY
Le sieur MARLET
ANTOINE ALLAIRE, employee for concession of
        Le Blanc
BELSAGUY, a widow
BERARD, jobber
Le sieur CANTILLON
SOULEVAIN
BERARD
DUMANOIR manager of St. Catherine grant at
        Natchez
HUCQ, a coppersmith, wife
HARDY, woman

                                    A-23

SOME COLONIST OF LOUISIANA MENTIONED
IN A LETTER BY DELACHAISE DATED OCTOBER 18,1723

Le sieur FAZENDE, second councillor
M. FLEURIAU
Le sieur DUVAL
Le sieur PITACHE, keeper of merchandise belong-
          ing to M. Law
COUSTILHAS
PAILLOUX
De GRAVES
Le sieur La MARQUE
Du COEDER
MAREST de la TOUR
BASSE
DALCOURT, cashier
GAUVRY
THIERRY
DUPUY PLANCHARD
de la LOERE the younger
DURAND
BONNEAUD
MANADET, surgeon
BRULE
PERRY
NOLAN
BAJOT
De LORME
BION
Le sieur DUPRE, captain of the ship Expedition
SABANNIER, plantation owner
De LOUBOEY
DE LA TOUR, lieutenant general died October 1723
Father RAPHAEL
BOISPINEL, second engineer at Mobile also died
De CHAVILLE, engineer returning to France
Le sieur de la SALLE, warehouse guard at Biloxi
La SALLE, surgeon at Biloxi
St. JEAN, soldier at Biloxi
BRESSAN, soldier at Biloxi
ADRIEN GILBERT, master carpenter on concession
          of DUMANOIR
Le sieur PAUGER, engineer
Le sieur GUERIN, arrived on the ship Expedition
Le sieur DUTERPUY

Le sieur DEVIN, draughtsman
BOISPINEL, engineer
DESLIETTES, of Natchez
PAQUIER, officer at Natchez
de CHEPART, officer at Natchez
Le sieur de GRAVES
Le sieur d'HERBANNE
Le sieur PECHON, commandant at Alibamons
Le sieur de la LANDE of Mobile
Le sieur MASCLARY
La PERRIERE
BELSAGUY woman in Mobile
ROSSARD, record clerk
TRUDEAU woman, wife of a carpenter

\* \* \* \* \* \* \* \* \* \*

CENSUS OF THE HABITANTS OF THE
GERMAN VILLAGES LOCATED TEN LEAGUES ABOVE
NEW ORLEANS ALONG THE RIVER, UNDER COMMAND
OF SIEUR D'ARENSBOURG  November 12, 1724

GERMAN VILLAGE OF HOFFEN

1. SIMON LAMBERT, age 40, native of Oberebesheim,
   Spire, laborer, wife, son age 18.
2. CONRAD FREDERIC, age 50, native of Rothemberg,
   spire, laborer, wife, 5 children including
   a boy of 5, a girl of 18.
3. JEAN GEORGE TROUSLER, age 26, native of Lichtem-
   berg, Alsace, mason, wife.
4. JEAN GEORGES POCH, age 38, native of Gobcher,
   Strausberg, weaver, wife, child.
                    Land abandoned by Conrad
                    Frederic and Simon Lambert.
5. GUILLE ZIRIAC, age 50, native of Ilmenstad,
   Mayance, laborer, former coachman to the
   King Stanislaus, wife, girl 7 years.
6. JEAN CALLENDRE, age 26, native of Aubrequin,
   Palatinate, laborer, wife, girl age 14,
   sister in law, mother in law.
7. ESTEBAN KISTENMACH, age 39, native of Cologne,
   wife, girl age 10.
8. JEREMIE WAGNER, age 27, native of Orensburg,
   d'Ansbach, Bavaria, laborer and hunter,
   wife, sister in law, child.
9. LEONARD MAGDOLFT, age 45, native Hermunse,
   Wurtemberg, laborer, wife, orphan boy
   10 who is adapted.
10. ANDRE SCHANZ, age 25, native of Hochausen,
    Franconia, miller, wife, child, step-
    daughter age 15
11. JEAN GEORGES PETZ, age 32, native of Weibstadt,
    Spire, butcher and prevost, wife, child,
    orphan girl age 9.
12. JEAN ADAM MATERNE, age 26, native of Rosenheim,
    Alsace, weaver, wife, child, two sister-
    in laws age 18 and 20.
13. GASPARD TOUBS, age 40, native of Zurich,
    Switzerland, laborer, wife, 2 boys age
    10 and 12, three others

A-24

14. AMBROISE HAIDEL, age 22, native of Neukirchen,
    Meyance, baker, wife, brother age 18,
    brother in law age 13.
15. JACQUES REITER, age 28, native of Lustuen,
    Wurtemberg, shoemaker, wife.
16. MICHEL VOGEL, age 40, native of Aldorf, Suevia,
    wife, boy age 2, girl age 18.
17. SEBASTIEN FUNCK, age 30, native of Hagenau,
    Alsace, Laborer, wife, child of 1 year,
    orphan girl age 16 years.
18. MICHEL HORN, age 39, native of Limbal,
    Mayence, laborer, wife, girl age 8.
19. abandoned land, reserved for the surgeon
    of the company.
                  Old german village located
        back from the river, November 13, 1724
20. BALTAZARD MONTHE, age 22, native of Troppau,
    Selecia, laborer, wife, girl 18 months.
21. JEAN GEORGES ROEZER, age 32, native of Biebrich,
    Mayence, blacksmith, wife, orphan girl
    age 18.
22. JEAN JACOB BEBLOQUET, age 36, native of Lamberloch,
    Alsace, laborer and hunter, wife, 3 children
    2 boys and 1 girl, age 13 yrs to 2 yrs.
23. JEAN FRIZMAN, age 46, native of Routh, Switzerland,
    laborer, wife, boy of 5.
24. BALTAZARD MARX, age 27, native of Wullenberg,
    Palatinate, wife age 22, a nailsmith.
25. BERNARD WICH, age 46, native of Tainlach,
    Wurtemberg, laborer, wife, 3 children
    1 boy, 2 girls ages 13 years to 2 months.
26. JEAN ROMEL, age 24, native of Kinhart,
    Paratinate, tailor, wife.
27. CATHERINE WELLERIN, age 49, native of Heilbronn,
    Wurtemberg, widow of Auguste Paur, 2 children.
28. ANNE COHN, widow of Jean Adam Zwike, laborer who
    died at Biloxi, dau 12 years.
29. MADELAINE FRONBERGER, age 50, widow of George
    Mahyer, laborer, native of Insitippil,
    Swabia, son age 20, orphan girl age 20.
30. MARGUERITTE REYNARD, native of Bauerbach,
    Baden, spire, age 46. Listed as wife of
    Johann Leuck, now separated. Girl age 7.
31. CATHERINE HENCHE, age 50, native of Horenbourg,
    Brandenbourg, widow of Cristian Grabert who
    died in Biloxi, girl age 14.
                    A-24

32. CRISTIAN GREBER , age 23, native of Brandebourg,
    Laborer, wife, orphan boy age 13.
33. ANDRE NEIKER, age 36, native of Dettenhausen,
    Wurtembourg, miller, wife.
34. JACOB OBERLE, age 33, native of Zabern, Alsace,
    weaver, wife.
                    Land in conflict between Neiker
        and Oberle_on one side, d'Arensbourg on the
        other.
                    The first old german village
35. ANDRE SENCH, age 35, native of Saxony, old prevost
    of the village and farmer, wife, child 2.
36. MARC TIL, age 43, native of Bergwies, silesia,
    shoemaker, wife.
37. MAURICE KOBEL, age 64, native of Berne, Swit-
    zerland, butcher. For 30 years served with
    the Swiss regiment in France , wife.
38. d'ARENSBOURG, retired captain, age 31, orphan
    boy age 12 or 10.
                    Following is a description of the
        lands of the German Coast and giving reasons
        for abandonment of certain sections, including
        flooding and huricanes.
39. ANDRE TREGUE, age 37, native of Donauwoerth,
    Bavaria, hunter, wife, child.
40. JEAN SENEK, age 45, native of Weissenberg,
    Laborer, separated from wife who lives in
    the village.
41. ANDRE HOFFMAN, age 27, native of Ansbach, Bavaria,
    Woodcutter, wife, girl age 7.
42. MATHIEU FREDERIC, age 29, native of Weilersheim,
    Alsace. Laborer, wife, child, orphan girl
    age 15.
43. BERNARD LAUESCH, age 52, native of Palatinate,
    tailor, wife. boy age 15 years, girl
    age 11.
44. PAUL KLOMP, age 30, native of Bauerbach, Baden,
    laborer, wife, boy age 2 orphan boy age 12.
45. The chapel and the cemetery
46. ADAM SMITZ, widower, age 44, native of Isnen,
    Suevia, girl age 9. He is a shoemaker.
47. JEAN RODDER, age 35, native of Rastadt, Baden,
    locksmith, wife.
48. ANTOINE TISTELZUE, age 29, native of Selz,
    Alsace, laborer, wife, child 1½.

49. GUILLAUME PICTOT, age 50, native of Morison,
      Brittany, laborer, wife.
50. FREDERIC MELQUET, age 40, native of Wurtemburg,
      butcher, wife.
51. PIERRE MUNICK, age 40, native of Oberheim,
      Palatinate, carpenter, wife, girl age 14,
      child 12 days old.
52. ANDRE STRIMPHLE, age 33, native of Ottersheim,
      Baden, wife, boy age 1 year.
53. JEAN ADAM REIL, age 45, native of Hatzweiler,
      Basle, Switzerland, carpenter, wife, girl
      age 5 months.
54. JACQUES POCHE, age 45, native of St. Omer in
      Artois, shoemaker, wife.
55. JOSEPH WAGUEPAK, age 23, native of Schwobsheim,
      Alsace, laborer, wife.
56. SIBILLE HEILE, wife of the dec. Weidel, age 37,
      native of Elchingen,  Suevia.
57. JEAN ADAM EDELMAYER, age 50, native of Reiheim,
      Palatinate, cooper, wife, 2 boys age 14 and 10.
58. PHILIPPE ZOUN, age 25, native of Grosshoeflein,
      Hungary, laborer, wife.
               Here is a passageway leading to
      the concession of M. de Meuirs.
59. JEAN JACOB FOLTZ, age 26, native of Ramstein,
      Palatinate, shoemaker, wife, child 1 year.
60. BERNARD AUTT, age 30, native of Wurtemberg,
      Laborer, wife, boy age 10.
               Concession of M. de Meures, on
      which is M. de LAIRE, a valet, women
      servants, and a child.
               Next is the Village of Taensa
               Following is the land of M.
      de la Harpe, along the river.

*  *  *  *  *  *  *  *  *  *

CENSUS OF HABITANTS ALONG THE
MISSISSIPPI RIVER FROM NEW ORLEANS TO
OUACHA, OR THE GERMAN VILLAGES,
COMPILED DECEMBER 20, 1724

1. JACQUES LARCHE, age 30, native Quebec, Canada,
    wife, 2 children, Bienville's land.
2. JEAN JOSEPH Le QUINTREE, age 27, native Bretagne,
    wife, Bienville's land.
3. GASPARD HECKLE, age around 35, native Switzerland,
    wife, girl, orphan boy, Bienville's
    land.
4. JACOB HOUBER, age 45, native Luabe ( Suabe?) a
    laborer, wife, 16 yr old boy, Bien-
    ville's land.
5. ANDRE KRESTMAN, age 45, native Augsbourg ( Bavaria),
    wife, 2 boys, age 16 & 18, orphan
    girl 15, another girl age 5, Bien-
    ville's land.
6. Le sieur ESTIENNE ROY, age 33, native Montreal,
    Canada, wife, Bienville's land.
7. SIMON KUHN, age 50, native Wissembourg (on the Rhine)
    wife, daughter, son of DANIEL YOPF
    living in household, age 25, an
    orphan age 12, Bienville's land.
8. widow MILHER, husband was a Brickmaker, he died 8
    years ago, 2 daughters age  14 and 3,
    Bienville's land.
9. JEAN WEYBER, age 28, native of Le Kelle, Strausbourg,
    Alsace, wife, neice, orphan girl age
    16, Bienville's land.
10. Concession of CLAUDE JOSEPH DUBREUIL, age 30, native
    of Dijon, Bourgogne, Came to La. in
    1719. Wife, 2 boys age 9 &11, one
    other age 17. Listed on his concession
    are the following persons:
    JACQUES MOREAU native of Paris, age 47
    PIERRE REFFAIT, Carpenter from Orleans
    JOSEPH LANGLOIS, Tailor
    ANTOINE JOSEPH deLATTES, joiner, from Doyai
    HENRY WAGON, native of Hainault ( Belgium)
    PIERRE PASSERA
    Also negroes, slaves, etc.

B-24

11. CHAUVIN de LERY, age 50, native Montreal, Canada,
                    3 boys age 13, 15, &11.
                       Listed on his land are:
            WILLARD, a carpenter
            BEAUPRE
            Negroes, slaves.
12. LOUIS CHAUVIN de BEAULIEU, Native of Montreal, Canada,
                    age 46, wife, a cousin, negroes, slaves
13. CHAUVIN de la FRESNIER, Native Montreal, Canada, age
                    48, wife, 3 children. Occupation,
                       Indigo grower. Listed on his land:
            BELLAIR
            LANGEVIN,     indigo grower
            MOUSSIGUAC
            De COUOUIE
            GIRAUD, joiner
            three orphans
14. On the concession of Ste Reyne:
            CEARD, Director
            DUPLESSIS, Alternate Director
            DALGUERAY, Employee
            widow FLOT, now wife of a storekeeper,
                       with 2 children
            CAUDIE, Master carpenter, with wife
            AURETAILL, joiner
            SOISSOUD, joiner
            DECOUS, silkgrower, with wife and child
            DUBOIS    carpenter
            Le JOYE and DAUBLIN, tailors
            POURCEAU, Stoneworker ( Prob. pottery), with
                       an orphan boy  age 17, 2 orphan
                       girls age 6 & 10
15. JOSEPH VERETTE, age 29, native Quebec, Canada, wife.
16. Concession of Comte d'Artagnan:
            D'ARTIGUIERE
            De BENAC
17. HENRY PELGRIN, laborer on d'Artagnan concession,
                    native Provence, age 25, wife,
                    2 children.
18. PELLERIN, employee of the company. In same household:
            ANDRE CREPE, age 25, native of Grace, Provence,
                    laborer for d'Artagnan concession, wife.
19. PIERRE COUSIN, age 38, native Vienne, Dauphine
                    wife, child. In same household:
            JACQUES GENETEL, age 52
            FRANCOIS DAUPHINE
                                        B-24

20. GUILLAUME VAQUIR, age 27, native Quercy, Aquitaine,
                wife, child of 2.
21. Concession of Diron, in his household are:
        DESJEAN, absent director
        MICHEL the young, age 17.
22. Concession of Comte d'Artagnan, at Cannes Bruslee
                On the concession are:
        D'ARTAGUIERE
        De BENAC
        Le Sieur BOUSSIGUAC, surgeon
        St. PATU, employee
        COUDERC, Carpenter
        IMBERT, Locksmith, wife.
23. CHANTREAU de BEAUMONT, wife, 4 children
24. JEAN PUJEAN, age 30, native of Lerac, Bordeaux.
                In the same household:
        JOSEPH HARASSE, Native of Paris, age 23, wife.
                Both work for concession of d'Artagnan.
25. CLAUDE MERAND, age 28, native of Paris, worker for
                concession of d'Artagnan.
26. DENIS FERANDON, native of Bourbonnais, wife. Worker
                for concession of d'Artagnan. In the
                same household:
        FRANCOIS MONGE
        EDME DOUNOU
27. SEBASTIEN BOUETTE, age 40, native Varade, Nantes.
28. FRANCOIS CHEVAL, age 35, native Dauphine, wife
                Laborer, concession of Dubuisson.
29. RENE CHESNEAU dit DUCHESNE, age 33, native of Anjou,
                wife.
30. PHILIPPE DAUNY, age 22, of Flanders, wife.
31. PIERRE BROUT, age 37, wife.
32. PIERRE POMMIER, age 24, native Belfort, Alsace, wife.
33. FRANCOIS PICOLLIER, age 22, native Daunoy, Savoy,
                worker for concession of d'Artagnan.
                In the same household:
        PIERRE CEZARD dit La BEYE, age 25, native of
                Brye, Seine, wife, child.
34. PIERRE SAINTON, Habitant of des Allemands, age 28,
                native of Chatellerant ( prob.
                Chatellerault, Vienne, Dauphine)
                wife, 2 children ages 4 & 2.
35. DIZIER, native of Marseille, worker for concession
                of Diron, 3 year old daughter.
36. Habitant of household of DEJEAN; director for the
                concession of Diron:

                                        B-24

PIERRE PELLOIN, age 40 or 45, native of Brinon,
Normandy, wife, laborer for concession
of Diron.

DIRON

37. PIERRE SMITH, age 34, native of the Palatinat, Rhine
valley, laborer. wife, boy age 17.

38. BARTHELEMY YENS, age 25, native Cologne, Rhine valley
wife, child.

39. Habitant of ST.PIERRE ST.JULIAN :
JEAN FRANCOIS DAUNY, domestic, with german
wife, orphan of 10 years.

REMY PIQUET

40. FRANCOIS GOBERT, age 28, native of Dieppe, Normandy
wife, child. Worker for concession
of Diron.

41. ANTOINE ROUX dit Le FLEUR, age 30, native of Castel-
naux, Provence, worker on concession
of d'Artagnan.

42. HENRY CANTION, age 25, native of Provence, wife,
worker, concession of d'Artagnan.

43. THOMAS GUICHARD, age 30, native of Lyon, Lyonnais,
wife, child age 10, worker on
concession of Ste. Reyne.

44. PIERRE PIQUERY, age 31, wife. Worker on concession
of Ste. Reyne.

45. Habitant of Mr. PETIT de LIVILLIERS, age 22, officer
from Canada.

46. DUCROS, age 35 or 40, native of Provence, wife.

47. BERNARD LANTHEAUME, age 50, native Valence, Dauphine,
his family is in France.

48. JOSEPH RITTER, age 52, native of Dourlac ( Dour,
Belgïum?)carpenter, wife, boy of 20,
2 orphans of 14 and 18.

49. CLAUDE BAILLIF, age 58, native of Picardy, wife,
girl age 18, a laborer.

50. JOSEPH BAILLIF, age 22, native of Lorainne, Germany ,
wife, laborer.

51. NICOLAS SMITZ, age 40, native Frankfort,Germany,
wife, laborer, 2 girls age 18 and 6.

52. PIERRE BAYER, age 23, native of Phillipsburg,
Germany, wife, laborer.

53. JEAN FOUX ( wishes to be called RENARD), age 38,
native of Bearn, Switzerland, wife,
daughter.

54. LAURENT RITTER ( the younger), age around 20, habitant
on Bayou st. John, of the habitation of

FRANÇOIS DUGAY

55. ESTIENNE DAIGLE, age 27, native Quebec, Canada,
    wife, 3 orphan children
56. LOUIS VIGIER, age 35, native Montreal, Canada,
    wife, child.
57. PIERRE RICHAUME,  age 26, native Quebec, Canada,
    wife, child.
58. JOSEPH LARCHE ( the younger), age 28, native Quebec,
    Canada.
59. JEAN CARON, age 25, native Picardy, wife, 2 children
    ages 2 & 3.
60. Habitant of M. de PAIJHOUX, Major General.

\* \* \* \* \* \* \* \* \* \*

## CENSUS OF HABITANTS OF DAUPHIN ISLAND, ALONG THE MOBILE RIVER, CAT ISLAND, AND PASCAGOULA, COMPILED MARCH, 1725 by M. GORTY.

### ISLE DAUPHINE

1. RENAULT, and another man
2. HERVIEUX, wife, 3 children

### MOBILE RIVER

3. La TOUR, wife.
4. BOURGUIGNON
5. TALON
6. LUSSER, wife, 2 children

### LES CHAETS ( Cat Island)

7. Du BREUIL, wife, 4 children
8. OLLIVIER, wife, 2 children
9. ROCHON, wife, 5 children
10. CATEL
11. MIRAGOIN, wife, 4 children
12. HUET, wife, 4 children
13. BARREAU, wife.

### PASCAGOULA

14. JOSEPH La POINTE, wife, 3 children
15. LAVERGNE
16. La MOTTE
17. GRAVELINE, 2 children
18. St. LAURENT, 1 child
19. BONON, wife
20. BRASSELIE. wife, 2 children
21. La GARDE
22. CRISHAN, wife, 2 children.

* * * * * * * * * *

A-25

MAP OF LOUISIANA
SHOWING THE SITES
OF FRENCH OCCUPATION
IN 1726-1727

To Akan-
sas and
Illinois

This section later
West Florida

To Mobile

N

Louisiana
swamps

1. Natchitoches
2. Natchez & Yazous
3. Oumas
4. Pointe Coupee
5. Baton Rouge
6. Bayogoula
7. Biloxi
8. Ouacha
9. Les Allemands
   ( German villages)
10. Chapitoulas

11. New Orleans
12. Boulaye
 3. Detour L'Anglais
    (English Turn)
14. Dezert
15. Petit Dezert
16. Tonicas
17. La Balize

A. Red river
B. Mississippi
   ( St. Louis)
   river
C. Lafourche R.
D. Iberville R.
E. L. Maurepas
F. L. Ponchar-
   train
G. L. Borgne
H. Pearl River
I. Gulf of
   Mexico

SCALE: 1" = 60 miles , english measure
      1" = 180 lieues ( leagues)
          French measure.

## NOTES ON THE CENSUS OF 1726

The census of 1726 is probably the most complete
for the period, including as it does all of French
Louisiana. As is indicated in this census, this
included the entire Mississippi valley, and the
French villages along the gulf coast.

The January, 1726 census gives totals as follows:

| | | |
|---|---|---|
| French citizens ( Masters) | 1952 | persons |
| Servants of european origin ( Engagees) | 276 | persons |
| Negro slaves | 1540 | persons |
| Indian slaves | 229 | persons |

These are numbered in the following pages in the right
hand columns by masters, servants, negro slaves, and
indian slaves. No number in a column or a zero indicates
no one in that household of that classification.

The original of this census also shows number of cattle
and amount of land under cultivation.

The copy of the census is signed by de Chavannes, who
was at the time secretary to the superior council in
Louisiana.

In October, 1726 the citizens requested through the
superior council that the Company supply 1863 negroes
for the future development of the colony. Although
most of the citizens requested five or six, there were
a few concessionaires who requested 30, 50, and even
100 negroes.  Although the number of negroes requested
appear in the original, these numbers were not copied
in this record. There is no indication that the request
was granted, or the number of negroes requested agree
with the number granted. The request includes notes
by the council showing the reason for the request and
the councils recommendation.

This record is a census in itself, albeit a census of
those people in the colony who were considered important
enough to receive special considerations from the company.

GENERAL CENSUS OF ALL INHABITANTS
OF THE COLONY OF LOUISIANA DATED JANUARY 1,
1726, INCLUDING THE ENTIRE COAST BORDERING
THE GULF OF MEXICO FROM MOBILE TO NEW ORLEANS,
COLONIES ALONG THE MISSISSIPPI RIVER, INCLUDING
THE REGION KNOWN AS ILLINOIS.

1. Land along the river, above New Orleans, alloted to
          M. de Bienville
     Habitation of M. de BIENVILLE:
     two nephiews of M. de BIENVILLE,
     Le sieur DEMOUY,                          3, 2, 4, 2
          German Vassals:
     GASPARD, wife, 2 children                 4, 1, 0, 0
     JACQUES ONNERE, wife, child               3, 1, 0, 0
     ANDRE SECREMENT, wife, 2 children         4, 2, 0, 0
     JACQUES IGOUETTE, forced immigrant        1, 0, 0, 0
     Le ROY, wife, et BELLAIR, assoc.          3, 1, 1, 0
     SIMON COMME, wife                         2, 2, 0, 0
     DANIEL GOPE, wife, child                  3, 0, 0, 0
     THOMAS LAISNE, wife                       2, 1, 0, 0
     ANDRE CREPE, wife, child                  3, 0, 0, 0
     JOSEPH VERRET, wife                       2, 2, 0, 0
     Le sieur BONNAUD, former
          company storekeeper                  0, 1, 8, 0
2. At Chapitoulas
     DULUDE, DECONOIRE, of the concession
     of St. Reyne, with 2 children             3,10,83, 0
     Le sieur DUBREUIL, concessionaire,
          wife, 2 children                     4, 5,48, 2
     Le sieur CHAUVIN de LERY,
          3 children                           4, 2,95, 2
     Le sieur CHAUVIN La FRENIER, wife,
          3 children                           5, 2,115, 3
     Le sieur CHAUVIN BEAULIEU, wife,
          3 children                           5, 2,44, 4
3. At Providence
     FRANCOIS LARCHE, wife, child              3,
     JEAN SOUDRES, wife, associate,
          1 child                              4,
     HENRY PELLEGRIN, wife, 2 children         4,
     PIERRE COUSIN, wife, 1 child              3,
     LOUIS LAMALATIE, associate                2,
4. At Cannes Brulees

                                        A-26

```
        Concession of M. DIRON              1, 2,23, 0
        Concession of M. le Comte d'Artagnan,
                Sieur de BENAC, Director 1, 3,29, 4
        FRANCOIS DAUPHIN, father,
                wife, child                  3,
        JOSEPH DAUPHIN, son, wife            2,
        JACQUES PUJAULT, wife                2,
        FRANCOIS CHEVAL, wife, 2 children 4, 1,
        RENE DUCHESNE, wife                  2,
        JACQUES POCHE, wife, associate       3,
        JOSEPH QUINDRE, wife, 2 children,
                associate                    5,
5. Village of Colapissas
        PHILIPPES DAFOU, wife, child,
                associate                    4,
        RENE BELLEAUDAU, wife, child         3, 1,
        La COSTE, wife, 2 children,
                associate                    5,
        PIERRE CEZAR, wife, 1 child          3,
        PIERRE POMMIER, wife, 2 children     4,
        AUGUSTIN GOUIR, wife, associate      3,
        PIERRE La MOURY, wife, associate     3,
6. Village les Oumas
        FRANCOIS COLIN, wife                 2, 0, 2, 3
        JEAN BARBEAU, wife, 2 children       4,
        La CHEVALIER                         1,
        PIERRE BARON, wife, child            3, 5,
7. At Pointe Coupee
        GABRIEL POULIN, wife                 2, 3,
        ALBERT Le GROS, wife, 2 children     4,
        ALBERT de CUIR, associate,
                3 children                   5, 1,
        FRANCOIS DOEGOIN, wife, 3 child-
                ren, associate named
                BEAUFILS                     6,
8. At the village of the Tonicas
        THOMAS RENCON, wife                  2,
        CHANTIN, wife, child                 3,
        PAUL GOURON, wife, child             3,
        PIERRE GERMAIN, wife, child          3,
        PIERRE Le MOIRE, wife                2, 1,
        JEAN RONDEAU, wife, child            3,
        PIERRE BARBIER, wife, 2 children     4,
        JACQUES DUPRE, wife, child           3, 1,
        NICOLAS HEBERT, wife, child          3,
        NICOLAS PAILLARD, associate          2, 2,
```

A-26

```
             PIERRE HAURY, wife, child           3, 1,
             JOSEPH CARTON, wife, 2 children     4,
             JEAN PEJRET, wife, 2 children       4,
             JOLICOEUR, wife, child, associate   4,
             ANDRE COURANT, wife, 3 children     5,
  9. At Bayougoula
             Concession of Paris Duverney
             M. de VERTEUIL, wife, sister &
                             M. Du BUISSON       4, 6,15, 1
 10. At the village called Allemands
             JEAN RAVILLE, wife                  2,
             SIMON LAMBERT, wife, child          3,
             CONRAD FREDERICK, wife, 5 children  7,
             JEAN GEORGE PECK, wife, with
                     JEAN GEORGE, wife, &
                     with associate, 1 child     5,
             BERNARD VIQUE, wife, 3 children     5,
             CLAUDE MAGRE, and mother            2,
             GUILLAUME QUERJAC, wife             2,
             JEAN CALENDRE, wife, mother, &
                     sister in law               4,
             BALTAZARD MARON, wife, child        3,
             ETIENNE RISTAMPER, wife, child      3,
             JEREMIE VAGNER, wife, sister        3,
             LEONARD MADOLSE, wife, child        3,
             ANDRE SEAUTREI, wife, 2 children    4,
             GEORGES PITOCH, wife, 2 children    4,
             JEAN ADAM, wife, 2 children,
                     sister in law               5,
             GASPARD TONK, wife, 2 children      4,
             AMBROISE KIA, wife, child,brother,
                     & brother in law            5,
             JACQUES RITRE, wife                 2,
             MICHEL TOQUET, wife, 2 children     4,
             SEBASTIEN TAISIG, wife, 2 children  4,
             MICHEL KONE, wife                   2,
             ANDRE FOREUR ( LOREUR?), wife,
                     2 children                  4,
             FREDERIK D'ARENSBOURG, Captain des
                     Allemands, wife, child      3, 1,
             ANDRE DARQUER, wife                 2,
             JEAN ROLLIN, wife                   2,
             BERNARD RODOCHE, wife, 2 children   4,
             PAUL KAMPLE, wife, child            3,
             ADAM SOBUL, daughter                2,
             MARCON THIEL, wife                  2,
```

A-26

```
JEAN ORISMAN, wife, 2 children        4,
FREDERICK MERQUELA, wife              2,
PITRE MUNIQUE, wife, child            3,
JEAN GEORGES ROZERE, wife, 3 child-
        ren, brother in law           6, 1,
JOSEPH VAGNEUR, wife, child           3,
ANDRE SAUMNEL, wife, child            3,
JEAN ADAM EDETMEN, wife, 3 child-
        ren                           5,
JACQUES RABELLE, wife, 4 children     6,
MATHIAS FREDERIK, wife, 3 children    5,
JACQUES TORETS, wife, child           3,
BERNARD OLNTE (?), wife, child        3, 1,
ANDRE HOKMAN, 2 children              3,
PHILIPPES JUIN, wife, child           3,
CRISTIAN GEABERT, wife, mother,
        sister, mother's sister       5,
```

11. Concession of M. De Meuves at Tincoas

```
        Le sieur DeLAIRE, director            1, 2,
        FRANCOIS SAINTON, wife, 3 children    5, 1,
        PIERRE CHEMIN, wife, child,
                brother                       4, 2,
        ST. JULIEN                            1, 1, 8,
        FRANCOIS MOULAYE, wife, child         3, 0, 0, 1
        ANTOINE Le ROUX                       1,
        JOSEPH BAILLIF, wife, child           3, 1,
        JEAN VERNAY, wife, 2 children         4, 1,
        LAURENSQUELLE, wife                   2,
        CLAUDE BAILLOU, wife, child           3,
        The habitation of M. Petit de
                Livilliers                    0, 1, 2, 0
        NICOLAS CHEMIN, wife, 2 children      4,
        JEAN FOUQUER, wife, child             3,
        JEAN CHERNE, wife                     2,
        ETIENNE L'AIGLE, wife                 2, 1,
        LOUIS TAGIER, wife, child             3,
        PIERRE RICHAUME, wife, 3 children     5, 1, 3, 0
        Le sieur L'ARCHE, wife, 2 child-
                ren                           4, 2, 3, 1
        La GOUBLAYE, wife, 2 children         4, 1, 2, 1
        The habitation of the desceased
                M. Pailloux, above that
                of La Goublaye                0, 0,15, 0
        The habitation of the Company in
        New Orleans, commanded by
                M. Perrie ( Perier)           0, 1,25, 0
                                              A-26
```

```
Another habitation of M. de Bienville
located 2 leagues from New Orleans
          on the river                1, 1,45, 0
Habitation of one named PROVENCHE
          EMMERY, wife                2, 1, 2, 0
La PIERRE, wife                       2,
PAUL, wife                            2,
BOURBEAU, wife, 2 children            4, 0, 4, 1
PLAISANCE, wife                       2, 0, 1,
Habitation of M. Perry
Habitation of M. Fazende
MARRY                                 1, 3,19,
BARRE                                 1, 0, 1,
BALCONS                               1, 0, 4,
COUSSINE, wife, 3 children            5,
BIGOT                                 1,
Widow TREPANIER, 5 children           6, 0,17, 2
LABRO, wife                           2, 0,16,
Concession of Ste Catherine,
          M. DUMANOIR, director       1, 0,20,
Concession of M. DASFELD              1, 0,23, 1
```
12. Habitations straight up the river ( Mississippi)
```
and along the River
DRAPEAU, wife, 4 children             6,
DESLAUS                               1, 0, 5
FRANCOIS CARRIER                      1, 0,30, 9
JOSEPH LAGNIER, with NICOLAS
          NOISER & his wife            3,
JACQUES CARRIER, wife                 2, 0, 4,
JOSEPH CARRIER, wife, 3 children      5, 0,13, 1
TIXERANT, wife, 4 children            6, 0,42, 6
BOYER                                 1, 2, 1,
CHEVAL                                1, 1,
Habitation of Sieur Brusle            0, 0, 2,
Le sieur GILLARD                      1, 1,
LENARD and his son                    2,
CHAMILLY                              1, 0, 3, 1
MANADE , wife                         2, 0, 9,
La LOIRE, & JOUSSEN, wife             2, 0, 5, 1
ROCHON                                0, 1, 3,
CHAPERON                              1, 0, 5,
La LIBERTE, wife                      2, 0, 6,
Habitation of M. de Mandeville        0, 1, 6, 1
Habitation of Sieur Raguet            0, 1,17,
Habitation of Marche brothers         0, 0, 4,
```

A-26

```
            RAPHAEL, free negro                    1,
            Le sieur DALCOUR, wife, child          3, 0,16, 0
            Habitation of sieur Dupuy
                      Planchard                     0, 1, 4, 0
            TRUDEAU, and his habitation            1, 0,25, 0
            COUSTILLAS                             1, 0,11, 0
            REXFENCO, wife, 2 children             4,
            DARBY                                  1, 2,11, 0
            Habitation of Sieur Chavannes          0, 0, 2, 1
            The brewery of the Dreux brothers      0, 2, 2, 0
13. Habitants of the area of Natchez
            Concession of Terre Blanche ( White Earth)
            and of M. le Marquis d'Asfeld,
            Le sieur BROUTIN, director             1, 7,31, 0
            Concession of Ste. Catherine of M. Collis
            (Kolly), and associates. M. de
                      LONGRAIS, director          1,12,25, 4
            Concession of PELLERIN, and his
                      associates                   2, 3, 4, 0
            Le PAGE, Concessionaire                1, 0, 2, 3
            CHANNEAU de BEAUMONT, 2 children       3,
            RENE PAPIN, wife, 2 children           4, 1,
            ETIENNE ELOY, wife, 3 children         5,
            JEAN ROUSSEAU                          1,
            HARDY VILLENEUVE, wife                 2,
            JACQUES Le FRET, wife                  2,
            MATHURIN GOUPILLA                      1,
            LAURENT HURLOT dit La SONDE            1, 1, 1, 0
            JEAN BARAN, wife                       2,
            GUIBANA dit BEAUSOLEIL                 1,
            LOUIS HENRY, wife, child               3,
            NOEL SOILEAU, wife                     2,
            GUILLAUME MARTIN dit La LANDE          1,
            SIMON MOUTAY, child                    2,
            MICHEL PINSONNEAU dit BIGNON           1,
            ANTOINE JURARD, wife                   2, 1, 2, 1
            JEAN ROUSSIN                           4,
            FRANCOIS FRETIN, wife, child           3,
            JEAN VERNET, wife, child               3,
            JEAN FLANDRIN, wife, 2 children        4,
            LOUIS CORDELIER, wife                  2,
            LOUER & MANSEAU, associates            2,
            ETIENNE RIVE, wife, 2 children         4,
            NICOLAS La COUR, wife                  2,
            MICHEL BEAU, wife                      2,
            SIMON BIDEAU                           1,
```

A-26

```
JEAN DEVEL, wife, 2 children          4,
JEAN FRANCOIS HAMBAR, wife            2,
JULIEN CHARTIER, wife, child          3,
JEAN CHIT,  german, wife              2,
ANSELME FOUCAULT, wife, child         3,
NICOLAS ROUSSEAU, child, associate    3,
LOUIS MIRAULT, wife,    child         3,
URBIN MORON, wife, 2 children         4,
SEBASTIEN FROUIN, wife                2, 0, 0, 1
JEAN DEPART, wife, 2 children         4,
JEAN DILON, wife                      2,
PHILIPPES DENTIN, wife                2,
GUILLAUME BOITET                      1, 1,
RENE HAYNAULT, wife                   2,
OLLOUIN RICHARD, wife, associate      3,
Vassals of the Terre Blanche (white earth)
        concession                    0, 9, 0, 0
Vassals of the concession of
        Ste. Catherine                0,10, 0, 0
Le sieur Raguet                       0, 0, 0, 0
14. Habitants of the place called Yasous
        ETIENNE PINNALAIN and wife,
                PEZE dit Le BLOUN, wife,
                Le COUVREUR           5, 0, 0, 0
15. Habitants of Illinois
        Habitation of M. de Boisbriant
                and of La Loire       0, 2,22, 0
        M. RENAUD                     1, 3,20, 0
        La CROIX, wife, 5 children    7, 0, 1, 0
        ROLLET, wife, 2 children      4,
        NEAU  (REAU?), wife           2,
        GIARD                         1,
        PREE, wife, 2 children        4,
        RICHARD                       1,
        CONTEMS, wife, child          3,
        RIEUPORT                      1,
        BARON, wife, child            3,
        BARBONNE, wife, child         3,
        CHAPU, wife                   2,
        LOISEL, wife                  2,
        HEBERT, wife                  2,
        SANS CHAGRIN, wife, 2 children 4,
        TABUS                         1,
        TIMONIER                      1,
        DUTROU, wife                  2,
        BOURGMONT                     1,
                                      A-26
```

```
BAPTISTE, negro                         0, 1, 0, 0
JOSEPH, a spaniard, wife, 2
            children                    4,
ANTOINE, a spaniard                     1,
BIRON, child                            2,
St. JEAN, wife                          2,
La FOREST                               1,
BECQUEL, wife, 2 children               4,
La LANDE the younger                    1,
PRADEL                                  1, 0, 2, 0
BARCELONE                               1,
Du SABLON, wife                         2,
Des ESSARTS                             1,
ROBILLARD, wife                         2, 0, 0, 1
DRAGON                                  1,
CHASSIN, wife, 2 children               4, 0, 0, 2
La JEUNESSE dit LEGROS                  1, 0, 0, 2
LA PLUME, child                         2, 0, 3, 0
BELLEGARD, 2 children                   3, 0, 1, 2
LANGEVIN, child                         2,
St. PIERRE, wife, child                 3,
LANTURLU, wife                          2,
GARDON, wife, child                     3,
ANTOINE, wife                           2,
CANAREL, associate                      2,
ROBIN, associate                        2, 0, 0, 1
DANIEL                                  1,
CAPTAINE, wife                          2, 0, 0, 1
St. JACQUES, wife, child                3,
PIERRE                                  1,
GOUVERNEUR & LE BRUN                     2,
BELHUMEUR; wife                         2,
MARIN, wife, child                      3,
DAUPHINE, wife, 2 children              4,
BEAUSEJOUR & CAMARADE                    2,
THOMAS                                  1,
BELLEROSE                               1, 0, 0, 1
Le NORMAND                              1,
TEXIER, wife, child                     3,
La POINTE, wife, child                  3, 0, 2,
IGNACE HEBERT                           1,
Old TURPIN, 2 children                  3, 0, 0, 1
2 jesuit and 2 curez missionarys        4, 2, 9, 2
GIRARDEAU, wife, child                  3, 1, 1, 1
MELIQUE, officer La JEUNESSE,
            wife, child, farmers        4, 1, 0, 1
                                        A-26
```

```
La FATIGUE, wife, 2 children         4, 1, 1, 0
Des VIGNES, wife, 2 children         4, 0, 5, 2
La LANDE, LAISNE, wife, 4
          children                   6, 1, 1, 4
Du LONGPRE, wife, 2 children         4, 3, 2, 4
CARRIERE, wife, 2 children           4, 1,11, 1
Old POTIER, wife, 4 children         6, 0, 1, 2
DESLAURIES, wife, child              3, 2, 0, 1
Young TURPIN, wife, 4 children       6, 2, 2, 2
BAILLARGEN, wife, 2 children         4, 3, 3, 2
COLLET                               1,
De LAUNAY, wife, 2 children          4, 1, 0, 2
LAMY, wife, 3 children, nephew       6, 1, 3,
MICHEL PHILIPPES, wife, 6 children   8, 2, 5, 3
St. PIERRE, wife, 2 children         4, 0, 2,
La SONDE, wife, child                3, 2, 0, 1
BOURBONNOIS, wife, 3 children        5, 0, 2, 5
LEONNARD BOSSEROT, wife, 4
          children                   6, 1, 7, 2
MERCIER, wife, child                 3, 1, 0, 0
OLLIVIER, wife                       2,
CLOUET, wife, 2 children             4, 1, 0, 1
POTIER the young, wife, child        3, 1, 4, 2
La RENAUDIERE, wife, 2 children      4,
MALET, wife                          2,
CADONNIER, wife                      2, 0, 1, 1
BEAUJOLY                             1,
La LANDE the younger, wife, 3
          children                   5, 1, 6, 6
FRANCHOME, officer and wife          2, 1, 6, 6
La RIGUEUR, wife                     2, 1, 3, 1
BIENNOM the younger                  1, 0, 0, 1
ADAM                                 1,
De NOYAN                             1,
GAUTIER, wife                        2,
HEBERT, wife                         2, 0, 1,
BOISSEAU, wife, 3 children           4,
LIBERGE                              1,
St. CERNAY                           1,
La BONTE, Tailor                     1, 1,
TAILLOUX, wife, 2 children           4,
PORTIE, wife                         2,
St. JEAN, wife, 4 children           6,
PIGNES, gunsmith                     1,
La VIGNE                             1,
Du LUDE                              1,
```

A-26

```
                PONDRES LAISNE                          1, 0, 0, 1
                Du LUDE, traveller                      1, 0, 1, 1
                VILLENEUVE, wife, child                 3,
16. Habitants of the Acansas, on the right, descending
        the river Mississippi
        Le sieur DUFRESNE, formerly of
                the concession of M. Law 1, 0, 0, 1
                PIERRE DOUY, wife                       2,
                BAPTISTE THOMAS, wife                   2,
                St. FRANCOIS, wife                      2,
                POITEVIN                                1,
                MONTPIERRE                              1,
                JEAN Le MIGNOU                          1,
                JEAN LOURS ( HOURS?)                    1,
                JEAN Le LONG                            1,
                BARTELEMIAS                             1,
                NOGUES                                  1,
17. Habitants on the Riviere Noire ( Black river)
        100 leagues from New Orleans
        Concession of  M. Le Marquis de Meziers,
        and Desmarches, situated on the Ouachita,
        M. DELAYE, director                     1, 7,20, 1
18. Habitants of Natchitoches
        M. de St. DENIS, Commandant,
                wife, 3 children                5, 2,10, 0
        M. de J. de ST. DENIS, in possession
        of land of the desceased
                CHARLES DUMONT                  0, 2,
        MALER, 3 children                       4, 0, 2,
        St. FRANCOIS, wife, MARION, wife,
                and associate                   4, 1,
        CHAGNAR, wife, child                    3, 1,
        La VERGNE, wife                         2,
        St. PIERRE, soldier, wife,
                2 children                      4,
        GUILLAUME BARBOT                        1,
        ALORGE PRUDHOME, wife, child            4,
        DAUPHINE, associate                     2,
        St. DENIS, wife, 3 children             5,
        ROLLAND                                 1,
        RONDIN                                  '
        PREVOFIVE, wife, child                  3,
        MAUBAUGE                                1,
        La TULIPE                               1,
        DUPIN, wife, 2 children                 4,
        KANTAIS, wife, associate                3,
                                                A-26
```

```
JOLYBOIS & DUBOIS, associates         2,
NICOLAS PREVOST, wife, child          3,
MARECHAL, wife, 2 children            5, 0, 1,
CHARDON, associate, 1 other           3,
CROMER, wife        2,
DROUILLON, wife, child                3,
CUSSON POUSSET, wife, associate       3,
JEAN DEFANCE                          1,
BOQUET                                1,
VERGER & La BOUCHERIE, associates     2,
PIEDHOME, wife, MEUNIER, wife,
          associates                  4,
Le BRUN, wife                         2, 0, 3,
St. LOUIS dit BLARD, wife             2,
COUTAIN, La FONTAINE & wife,
          associates                  3,
DUPLESSIS & TOURANGEOR, associates    2, 0, 1, 1
DERBANNE, wife, 4 children            6, 0,15,
SENS SANS, ETABLISSENT, & LIEU        4,
```

19. Village of Anoiettes
```
          The sieurs MESPLET, three masters,
          ten engagees, one child, names
          unknown                         4,11, 0, 0
```
20. Habitants of a small village called Chantilly,
          half a league from New Orleans
```
          The brothers DREUX              2, 3, 7, 2
          PASSEPARTOUT, wife, 3 children,
              2 sisters                   7,
          SANSON, wife                    2, 1,
          JEAN CASTEMBOURG, german, wife  2, 1,
          SOUBAGNIE, wife, 3 children     5, 1,
          LINET, wife                     2, 0, 1,
```
21. Habitants along the Bayou St. John
```
          LANGLOIS LAISNE, wife, 2 children 4, 0, 5, 1
          FRANCOIS DUGUE                  1, 0, 4, 1
          RINARD, wife, 7 children        9, 0,19, 1
          JOSEPH GERARDY, wife, 5 children 7, 0,13, 2
```
22.  Habitants along the road to New Orleans
          from the Bayou st. John
```
          M. GAUVRIT, Captain, wife,
              2 children                  4, 0, 3, 1
```
23. Habitants of Billoxy
```
          Warehouse of the Company        0, 0, 5, 0
          Widow ARLU, 4 children, sister  6, 0, 8,
          A gunsmith, a commissioner      2,
```

24. Habitants along the Pascagoula River
        Concession of Chaumont,

| | |
|---|---|
| Le sieur LAGARDE, director | 1. 2,22, 0 |
| La POINTE, wife, 2 children & | |
| La PRADE, wife, associate | 6, 0, 4, 8 |
| La VERGUE, wife, child | 3, 0, 4, |
| GRAVELINES, 2 children | 3, 0,19, 2 |
| La MOTTE, 2 children & DENIS, | |
|       Associate | 4, 0, 5, 2 |
| St. LAURENT | 1, 0, 2, |
| LOUIS BRASSELIER, wife, child | 3, |
| FONTAINE, wife | 2, |
| FRANCOIS RIEUX | 1, |
| LOUIS BOUDIGEON, wife, child | 3, |

25. Habitants of Isle Dauphine

| | |
|---|---|
| St. JEAN ARNAUD, & son | 2, 0, 7, 2 |

26 Habitant of Oyster Point (Pointe au Huitre)

| | |
|---|---|
| GUILLAUME HUET, wife, 4 children | 6, 0, 4, 1 |

27. Habitant of the d'Herbanne River

| | |
|---|---|
| BARON, wife | 2, 1, |

28. Habitants of Mobile

| | |
|---|---|
| NICOLAS BOUDIN dit MIRAGON, | |
|           wife, 3 children | 5, 0, 4, 2 |
| Warehouse of the Company | 0, 0,27, 0 |
| M. DIRON, Commander | 1, 1, 3, 3 |
| M. de BEAUCHAMPS, Major | 1, 0, 1, 1 |
| M. de LOUBOEY, Captain | 1, 1, 1, 1 |
| M. VITRAC de la TOUR, wife, | |
|        3 orphans | 5, 3,23, 4 |
| M. MARCHANT | 1, 0, 0, 5 |
| M. LUSSER, Lieutenant, wife, | |
|       5 children | 7, 1, 9, 3 |
| Le sieur BENOIST | 1, 0, 4, |
| Le Reverend Priest CLAUDE, | |
|       Capuchin | 1, |
| Le sieur La LOIRE FLANCOUR, | |
|       Principal Commissary | 1, 0, 0, 2 |
| NAVARRE, Surgeon Major | 1, 1, 1, 0 |
| DURAND, Commissary | 1, 0, 1, |
| VAUTIER, 2nd. Surgeon, wife | 2, 0, 0, 1 |
| Widow LA SUEUR, and her sons | 2, 0, 5, 1 |
| OLLIVIER, wife, 2 children | 4, 0,15, 4 |
| CLAUDE PARENT, wife, 2 orphan | |
|       children | 4, 0, 4, 3 |
| widow Le FAURE, 4 children | 5, 0, 2, 3 |

A-26

```
PASQUIER, tailor, wife,
        2 orphan children        4, 0, 0, 2
ROBERT TALOIS, wife, 2 children  4, 0, 2,
JEAN BON, wife                   2,
ETIENNE FIEURE, wife             2,
LAURENT MARTIAL, wife, 1 orphan  3,
ANTOINE TRENOIS, wife, 2 children 4, 0, 0, 1
JEAN HAYNAUD, wife, 2 children   4,
FRANCOIS ALLERN                  1, 0, 2, 2
PIERRE ROUSSEAU dit ALLAIN,
        wife, 2 children         4,
Mother of ANTOINE HUCHE, his wife,
        child                    3,
RONGER                           1,
NICOLAS MEUNIER dit VERSEILLES
        wife, 3 children         5, 0, 0, 1
PIERRE DAUMAILLE, wife, child    3,
RENE SABOURDIN, wife             2,
THOMAS FLEURY, wife              2,
PIERRE AUSY dit FRANCOEUR, wife  2,
widow FINO, 5 children           6,
JEAN BAPTISTE BEAUVAIS, wife     2,
NOEL PROVON, wife, child         3, 0, 1,
PIERRE RHEIMS, wife              2,
PIERRE HUBERT dit DUPLESSIS,
        wife, 2 children         4,
FRANCOIS St. AGNAN, wife         2, 0, 2,
BALTAZARD BARTHELEMY, wife,
        4 children               6, 0, 0, 1
TRANCHEMONTAGNE, wife, 2 children 4,
LOUIS BOURBON, wife              2,
IGNACE PETIT                     1,
GABRIEL DUYMAIS                  1,
FRANCOIS VILLEGER                1,
FELIX LURAS, wife, child         3,
JEAN PIERRE De VAUX, wife        2,
ANDRE BONNEUIL                   1,
JACQUES DUBOIS                   1,
LOUIS TALON, wife, child         3,
BARTHELEMY DHNIE, wife, child    3,
LOUIS BIGNON, wife, child        3,
JEAN CARMOUCHE                   1,
ETIENNE DuBORDIOUS, wife         2, 0, 6, 1
JOANNIS dit BELLEROSE, wife      2,
ROBERT JACOB                     1,
```

A-26

```
JEAN BAPTISTE HERNIAUX, wife,
          4 children                6,
FRANCOIS TAIBRE, wife, child       3,
PIERRE MOREL, wife                 2,
JEAN BIGORRE                       1,
MOUTON                             1,
RENE CHENIER                       1,
NICOLAS CHARPILLON, wife           2,
JACQUES DURTEAUX                   1,
BEAUREGARD                         1,
La FRANCE, wife                    2,
BELLEROSE, wife                    2,
BOULONNOIS, wife, 6 children       8. 0. 4,
FONTAILLES, wife, 4 children       6,
La MARRE, wife                     2,
RAYNAUD, wife                      2,
La TOUR, wife                      2,
CONTANT, wife                      2,
La DOUCEUR, wife, child            3,
JAVAL, wife                        2,
St. JACQUES, wife, child           3,
CHARDEL, wife                      2,
PAUL, wife, child                  3,
St. MARTIN, wife, child            3,
JOLYCOEUR, wife                    2,
L'EVEILLE, wife                    2,
La BUTTE, wife                     2,
St. CRUX, wife, child              3,
DAMEL, wife                        2,
COSNARD, wife, 2 children          4,
ANTOINE St. JACQUES, wife,
          3 children               5,
BEAULIEU, wife, child              3,
RENAUD, wife, 3 children           5,
DUPONT, wife, child                3,
TARASCON, wife, 2 children         4,
BURAT, wife                        2,
St. VINCENT DOURLIN dit DUBREUIL,
          wife, 4 children         6, 0,12, 2
BUBULE                             1,
ROCHON, wife, 5 children           7, 0,15, 7
GUILLAU THIBAUD, wife, child       3,
LOUIS De FLANDRE                   1,
GABRIEL de CAUSSE                  1,
```

29. Habitants of Allibamons
    La LANDE, Warehouse guard          1,
    MELIZAN, surgeon, not with the
            garrison                   1,
30. Habitants of La Balize
    Le sieur DUVERGER, Engineer        1,
    P. GASPARD, Gunsmith               1,
    Sieur St. MICHEL, Commissary       1,
    OLLIVIER, Surgeon                  1,
    11 workers, 31 negroes             0,11,31, 0

31. Census of the town of New Orleans arranged by
    residence in order on the streets on which
    they reside.
31-A. Rue du Quay ( Street of the warves)
    The Hospital, which has 3 nurses, and includes
    the habitation of M. PRAT, Doctor, a gardener,
    a washerwoman,  and two negro  men and two
    negresses.                        0, 5, 4, 0
    Le sieur MASSY. house for his
            employees when he is
            not on his plantation     0, 0, 0, 0
    Le sieur RAGUET, wife, 3 children 5, 0, 2, 0
    Le sieur D'ARTAGUETTE & THIERRY,
            Combined housing          2,
    Le sieur DUPUY, ensign, wife      2, 0, 1, 0
    La Direction, or the lodging of
            M. PERRAULT and his 2
            commissioners             3, 1, 3, 0
    Le sieur DUVAL, wife, child       3, 0, 3, 1
    BELLEGARDE, baker, and pensioned
            employee named CONIAIN    2, 0, 2, 0
    The DREUX brothers, when they
            are in town               0, 0, 0, 0
    MATHURIN ROY, Smith               1,
    REBOUL , hunter                   1, 0, 0, 1
    M. de  PAUGER, engineer           1, 1, 4, 0
    TIXERAN, his habitation when in
            town                      0, 0, 0, 0
    Sieur BONNAUD, former warehouse
            guard, wife, child        3, 1, 0, 0
    Widow TRUDEAU, 6 children         7,
    Le sieur De NOYAN, town house     0, 0, 0, 0
    Le sieur PETIT de VILLIERS, wife  2, 0, 2,

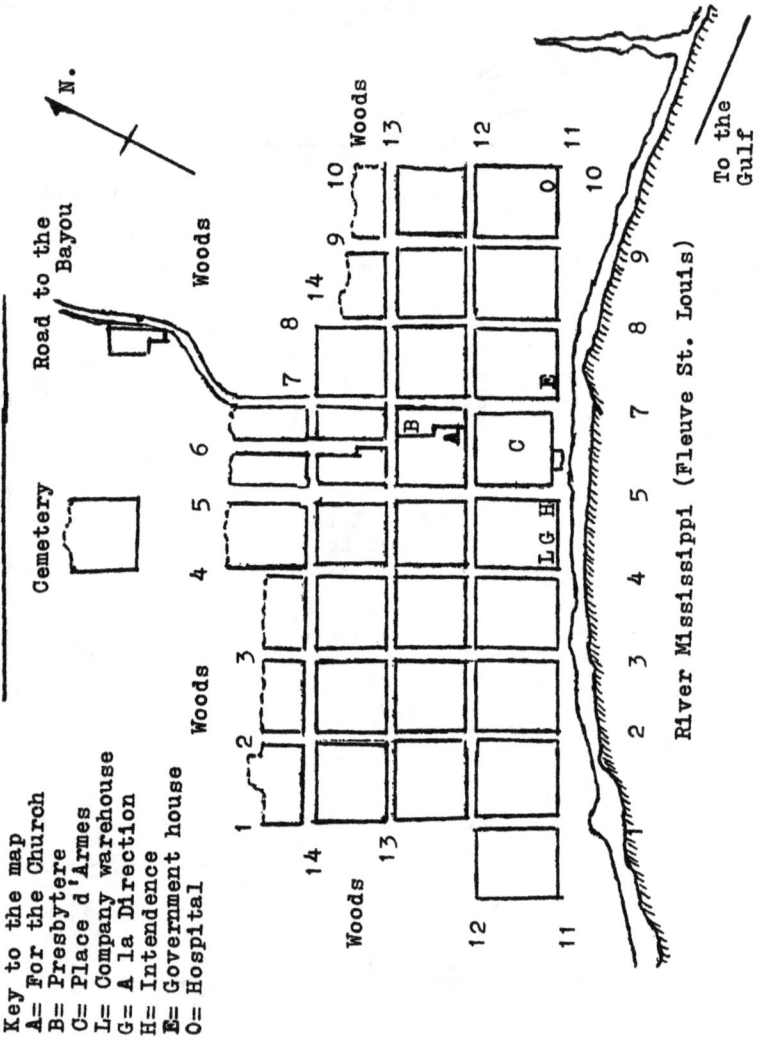

NEW ORLEANS FROM 1725 -1727

Key to the map
A= For the Church
B= Presbytere
C= Place d'Armes
L= Company warehouse
G= A la Direction
H= Intendence
E= Government house
O= Hospital

River Mississippi (Fleuve St. Louis)

To the Gulf

Road to the Bayou

Cemetery

Woods

N.

A-26

NEW ORLEANS FROM 1725 - 1727, Map and guide

11-11 The quay. No street, the land between the buildings
and the river reserved for wharves and business
purposes. On the west end of the city was the lands
of M. de Bienville.

12-12 West of the church the street is called Chartres,
the name borne by the entire street today. East
of the church the street was called Conde.

13-13 Royal street.

14-14 Bourbon street.

1-1 Bienville street. The 1726 census calls this street
Rue d'Anguin but lists no residents.

2-2 Conti street. The 1726 census calls this street
Bienville street.

3-3 St. Louis street.

4-4 Toulouse street.

5-5 St. Peter street.

6-6 From Royal street toward the woods only, called
Orleans street. The street never extended to the
river.

7-7 St. Anne street. Continuation of this street during
this period was the road to the Bayou St. John,
the "portage" for carrying goods from the Bayou
to the river.

8-8 Dumaine street.

9-9 Clermont street ( Clairemont). Now called St. Philip.

10-10 St. Adrien street. Now called Ursulines. In the
1725-1726 period this street was sometimes called
Rue d'Arsenal, and at this time was the eastern
extent of the city.

A-26

31-B. Rue de Chartres ( Chartres Street)
   ( Present Chartres Street from St. Peter
    to the present Bienville Street)
   House belonging to the Jesuits,
      at present vacant   0, 0, 0, 0
   House belonging to the Ste Reine
      Concession, occupied by
      M. De la CHAISE, wife,
      2 children, a commissioner
             4, 2, 1, 1
MORAND, wife       2, 1, 2
De BLANC, Major     1, 0, 2, 1
MICHEL SERINGUE, carpenter
    wife, child    3,
M. CEARD        1, 1, 1,
M. BRUSLE, concessionare
    wife, sister in law 3, 1, 2,
M. de MANDEVILLE, wife, 2
    children     4, 0, 2, 1
M. PERRY, Concessionare, and a
    commissioner   2, 1, 2
PREVOST, bookkeeper   1, 2,
CARITON, tailor, wife, child 3, 1,
FINDOR, traveler & JOSEPH DUCRO,
    wife, child    4, 0, 0, 1
Le sieur SARAZIN, former warehouse
    guard, wife, 3 children 5, 0, 2
St. MARTIN       1, 0,17, 1
DUVAL, and 3 canadian travellers 3,
Le sieur MAREST de la TOUR,
    and brother    2, 1, 1,
Le sieur ROSSARD, Court Notary
    and commissioner  2,12,
COUV. Boy employed by warehouse,
    CLAIRFONTAINE, employee,
    & TESSON, traveller 3, 1,
BELLAIR, day worker, wife,
    3 children    5, 0, 1,
AUFRERE, wife, child   3,
THOMELIN, joiner, 2 children 3,
BRUSLE, wife, 2 children  4,
An empty house belonging to the
    concession of D'Artagnan 0, 0, 0, 0

31-C. Rue de Conde ( Conde Street)
    ( Present Chartres Street between
     St. Ann and Ursulines)

| | |
|---|---|
| OZANNE & PANNETIER, coopers | 2, |
| Small house belonging to JOSEPH CARRIERE where he stops when he comes to town | 0, 0, 0, 0 |
| Le sieurs LAFONS, Brothers, surveyors | 2, 0, 0, 1 |
| DUVAL CHEVREUIL, goldsmith, & THOMAS ANULIN, wife, a hunter | 3, 1, |
| JEAN CARON, baker, wife, child | 3, 4, |
| CHAPRON on his plantation, house occupied by JOSEPH MOREAU, locksmith, wife, 3 children | 4, 1, |
| M. de BOISBRIAND, commandant, his nephiew & secretary | 3, 1, 0, 6 |
| BUSSON, indigo grower | 1, |
| VILLEURS, billiard keeper | 1, |
| Le FRERE MALO, tailor, & LOUIS Le DAIN | 2, 0, 0, 3 |
| PROVENCHE, wife | 2, |
| House belonging to CABASSIER, desceased, occupied by St. LAURENT, wife | 2, |
| Widow DRILLAND, 2 children | 3, 0, 1, |

31-D. Rue Philippes ( Now St. Philip Street)

| | |
|---|---|
| CHESNEAU, Cannonier of the village, 2 children | 3, 1, |
| JOSEPH, Day workman, wife, 2 children | 4, |
| ETIENNE BARROSSON, Blacksmith, wife, child and JACQUES VEILLON, turner | 4, |
| DUPONT, wife. | 2, |
| NICOLAS GUIDON, traveller, wife, child | 3, |
| LOUIS COLET, wife, child, & widow LAFOND | 4, |

31-E. Rue de l'Arsenal ( Arsenal Street)
    ( This street is now Ursulines Street)

| | |
|---|---|
| La VIOLETTE, traveller, wife | 2, |
| widow CHRISTINE de la VALLIE, her daughter, & FRANCOIS Le CLEF, her present | |

A-26

```
                    husband, a sailor        3,
        JEAN SIMON, wife, child              3,
        RENE MALIN, wife, child              3,
31-F. Rue Royalle ( Royal Street)
        M. CHEPARRE                          1,
        LAURENT                              1,
        JEAN RESNAU, day workman,
              wife, child                    3,
        REMY BIGEON, dit LA VIOLETTE,
              wife, child, and
              GILLES, hunter                 4,
        ANTOINE MICOU, Carpenter, wife       2,
        JACQUES GOUY dit St. ANDRE,
              wife, 2 children               4,
        GRACE, hunter, wife                  2, 2,
        JEAN MERLE, distributor of
              rations                        1,
        VINCENT HUISSIER, wife               2-
        DIZIER, wigmaker, wife, 2 children   4, ',
        NICOLAS FISSEAU, wife, 2 children    4,
        BONNAVENTURE, wife, 2 children       4, 1,
        THOMAS DEZERY, carpenter             1, 0, 4, 2
        La FLAMME, day workman, wife         2,
        MARTIN GODART                        1,
        GUILLAUME BLANVILLAIN, BARTHELEMY
              MACKIE, wife, child            4,
        LOUIS BROUET, wagonmaker, wife       2,
        NOEL AUBERT, chandelier, wife,
              child                          3,
        JOSEPH PETITCHARD, wife, child       3,
        LUE POIRIER, gunsmith, wife          2,
        LOUISE BOUREL, widow & GILLES
              LEMIRE, 2 children             3,
        YVES ONET, sailor, wife              2,
        FRANCOISE PORTIER                    1,
        JOSEPH BOISDORE, tailor, PIERRE
              POITEVIN, wife                 3,
        JEAN PASCAL, former employer,
              wife, child                    3,
        JULIEN BINARD, smith, wife           2,
        GUILLAUME LEMOINE dit Le NORMAND,
              Employer, wife, child          3,
        NICOLAS PORTIER, joiner, wife        2,
        JEAN MANSIERES, employer, wife,
              child                          3,
```

```
PIERRE PITIN, wife, child               3,
La RAQUETTE, sailor                     1,
MARIE BEAUREGARD                        1,
JEAN NANER dit PLAISANCE, child         2,
DENIS FERNAUDOU, wife, &
          FRANCOIS DUNALIE              3,
JACQUES FRANCOIS JAQUET, wife,
          child                         3,
The reverend priest Capuchin
          missionaries, residence       3, 0, 1, 1
PIERRE PLOUIN, workman                  1,
PIERRE PONSSELLE, tailor                1,
CLAUDE FONTAINE, traveller, wife,
          2 children                    4,
Widow La FAURE, 2 children              3, 1,
St MICHEL, employee of the
          company                       1,
LOUIS JARRY, innkeeper, wife,
          child                         3, 1,
The wife of GUILLAUME PERRIER, commander
          of the company's plantation,
          child                         2,
SULPICE L'EVIQUE, locksmith,
          wife, 3 children              5, 0, 0, 1
SANS SOUCY, traveller, wife             2,
BARBEJOUANNE, child                     2,
Le VEUF, shoemaker, wife,
          2 children                    4,
NICOLAS PIERRON                         1,
Madam ALORGE, widow of GRANDCHAMP,
          child                         2,
widow CANDEL, 2 children                3, 0, 4,
JEAN COUPART, joiner, wife,
          2 children                    4,1,
Le sieur ROGER, wife                    2,1,0,1
Large house belonging to Sieur
          CHAUVIN de la FRENIERE
          when he comes to town         0, 0, 0, 0
M. FAZENDE, concessionaire, wife,
          child, mother in law,
          brother in law                5, 0, 2,
DANVILLE, wife, child, & St. MARIE,
          employee on pension           4, 1, 1,
House belonging to Le Sieur
          DUPUY PLANCHARD, vacant       0, 0, 0, 0
```

```
          Le sieur BRU, Cashier              1, 0, 1,
          Le sieur St. QUINTIN, employee     1, 0, 1,
          M. Le sieur ETIENNE, former
                    warehouse guard          1, 1,
          Madame ( or widow?) SYLVESTRE      1, 1,
31-G. Rue de Bourbon ( Bourbon Street)
          FRANCOIS TRIBOULET, former sailor 4,
          Le sieur Du TOUR, employee         1, 1,
          GASPARD DIDIER, joiner, wife,
                    2 children               4,
          CHARLES GOUBIN, workman            1,
          ANTOINE CARON, employer, wife      2,
          JEAN BAPTISTE BARRE, wife          2,
          FRANCOIS CHEROPECHEUR              1,
          FRANCOIS Le FLOT                   1,
          La FLEUR, wagon maker              1,
          JACQUES GUYON, wife                2,
          JOSEPH Le CHAM dit LA ROSE,
                    wife, child              3,
          RENE PERE, Marshal                 1,
          TOINETTE GENEST, child             2,
          ANTOINE BUNEL, wagon maker, wife,
                    child                    3,
          FRANCOIS BOURDON, carpenter,
                    wife, 3 children         5,
          Le sieur JACOB, employee and his
                    daughter in law          2,
          widow De LAISTRE, child            2,
          La BOUILLONNERIE dit La DOUCEUR
                    wife, 3 children are
                    returning to France      5, 1,
          PIERRE BERNARD, wife               2,
          NICOLAS FRANCOEUR wife             2,
          DANIEL RAFFEAU, wife, roofer       1,
          JACQUES COQUELIN dit La FORME,
                    wife, child              3,
          ETIENNE DURAND dit DURANTE,
                    wife, 3 children         5,
          FRANCOIS FRIQUET, wife, child      3,
          MICHEL BROSSET, surgeon            1, 1, 0, 1
          NICOLAS BRANTON, Gunner for the
                    Company                  1,
          PIERRE PIVET, Gunner for the
                    Company                  1,
          POUYADON de la TOUR, surgeon       1, 2,
```

A-26

```
ANTOINE NEGRIER, wife                   2,
DUMESNIL, traveller, wife, child
        returning to France             3,
MARTIN DUCHATEAU & NICOLAS DUIRE,
        shoemakers                      2,
ANTOINE COMMERCY, cutter                1,
NICOLAS XAVIER, wife, child             3.
ETIENNE BEAUEOUR, hunter, wife          2,
MARIE MAGDELEINE BACHELET,
        4 children                      5,
GUILLAUME GUITON, baker, child          2,
FRANCOIS ALIX dit La ROSE, brewer,
        wife, child                     3,
FRANCOIS CANALLE, carpenter, wife 2,
Le sieur BION, & De MONTARGES,
        employees                       2, 1,
LOUIS PHILIDOR dit St. HILAIRE,
        carpenter, wife,
        2 children                      4, 0, 1,
MARIE LANDREAU                          1,
FRANCOIS MANSION, traveller, wife 2,
JEAN MERTUIS dit DAUPHINE, wife         2,
CLAUDE DONNEY, caulker, wife,
        2 children                      4,
JACQUES VALLERAND, turner, wife,
        child                           3,
ANDRE BERTOT, carpenter, wife           2,
Le sieur MESNARD, former employee
        of a concession                 1, 1,
NICOLAS GOUMY, mason, wife,
        2 children                      4,
BASTIEN LEGUIN, CLAUDE MARTIN,
        JACQUES SELAIN, & PIERRE
        Le COMTE, workmen living
        together                        4,
JEAN BAPTISTE BERGERON, wife            2,
Le sieur TRONQUIDY, wife, child         3, 1,
JACQUES SAUNIER, wife                   2,
GRACIEN LAUTIER, wife, 2 children 4,
PIERRE PIGUERE, baker, wife, child3,
widow GUYOT, child                      2,
FRANCOIS VITREQUIN, wife, 2
        children                        4,
CLAUDE DIDIER dit La PIERRE, wife 2,
PAUL Le BLEU, wife, child               3,
```

```
                PIERRE PETIT, wife, child           3,
                THOMAS GUICHARD, wife, child        3,
31-H. Rue de Bienville (.Bienville Street)
                Le Sieur de CHAVANNES, secretary
                    to the council                  1,
                M. FLEURIAU, Attorney General,
                        wife, sister                3, 0, 3,
                Habitation of JACQUES CARRIER,
                        presently on his
                        plantation                  0, 0, 0, 0
                Le sieur GOULAS, former swiss
                        officer                     1, 1,
                FRANCOIS BRACHON, wife, child       3,
                FRANCOIS GAGNE, wife                2,
                RODOLPHE MARTIN, wife, 2 children   4,
                TOUSSAINT BONVALIER, wife,
                        2 children                  4,
                JACQUES RICHARD, wife               2,
                DAVID, joiner, wife, brother        3,
                ETIENNE PATRAY & DAVID BILLON       2,
                Le sieur ALEXANDRE, surgeon major
                        of the hospital             1, 0, 1,
                JEAN VIT, joiner, son               2,
                JEAN FRANCOIS MANARD                1,
                MARTIN LANTIER, joiner, wife,
                        child                       3,
                JEAN BAPTISTE LANTIER, joiner       1,
                MORICE CANOT, wife                  2,
                NICOLAS CHRISTINE, Joiner, wife,
                        child                       3,
31-I. Rue St. Louis ( St. Louis street)
                GILLES ANOT, wife, child            3,
                THERESE PICHOT                      1,
                SEBASTIEN LARTAUT, tailor, wife,
                        child                       3,
                EDME SOUPART dit La FLEUR,
                        traveller                   1,
                FRANCOIS St. AMAND, former employee
                        of a concession, wife,
                        2 children                  4, 0, 0, 7
                TOINETTE FRAMBERT, wife of
                        PENIGAULT COUTURIER         1,
31-J, Rue Toulouse ( Toulouse street)
                CLAUDE COURTIN, JACQUES LE.FEVRE,
                JEAN DROU, FRANCOIS LOISEAU,
```

A-26

```
          and MARC Le GAUFRE, all sailors    5,
          JEAN COSTIER, carpenter, wife       2,
          HONORE ROTURIAU, miller             1,
          PIERRE CARMES, wife, child          3,
          CHARLES DUPONT, wife                2,
          CLAUDE HUE boiler maker, wife       2,
          NICOLAS CARDON, wagon maker, wife,
               child & VINIANTE,
               fisherman                      4,
          JOSEPH BREDA, wife                  2,
          ANTOINE ALLARD dit POSTILLON,
               wife                           2,
          LOUIS ROUSSEAU, wife, 2 children    4,
          LOUIS CORNEILLE, tailor             1,
31-K. Rue St.Pierre ( St. Peter street)
          MORISSET & HUET, former
               employees                      2,
          wife of CHAMILLY, 5 children        6,
          widow SAUSSIER, 5 children          6, 0, 1
          widow LA SALLE, child               2,
          ANDRE ROCHE dit TRANCHEMONTAGNE,
               wife                           2,
          MATHURIN SEIMARD,sailor, wife       2,
          NICOLAS DROUET, hunter, wife,
               child                          3,
          JACQUES ROBERT, wife, 3 children    5,
          MARTIN JACQUILLON, sailor, wife     2,
          PIERRE COUSSOT                      1, 0, 0, 1
          JOSEPH TERRIER, wife, &
               GUILLAUME DIEU                 3,
          PITACHE ( Le Sieur), employee,
               wife, child                    3,
          JACQUES DUPRE, joiner, wife         2,
          FRANCOIS MOREAU, wife               2,
          JEAN MOLET dit La RIVIERE, wife     2,
31-L. Rue St. Adrien ( St. Adrien street)
          (This street.is part of the street
          now called Ursulines)
          CARPENTRAS, carpenter, wife, child3,
31-M. Rue de Clermont ( Clermont Street)
          ( This street is now part of the
          street called St. Philip)
          RENE TOUCHE, wife,                  2,
          VINCENT, day workman                1,
          La GUIDON                           1,
```

31-N. Rue Dumaine ( Dumaine Street)
       BEAUME, canadian, wife,
           3 children           5,
       JEAN BIGNARD, cooper, wife, child 3,
       CONTOIS, lime maker, wife, child  3,
31-O. Rue St. Anne ( St. Anne street)
       BODSON, smith             1, O, 1,
       La TREILLE, cooper, wife      2,
       JARDELA, wife, 2 children     4,
       MARGUERITE La PROVENCALLE    1,
       BOURGUIGNON, locksmith, wife    2,
       LAZON, captain of a small vessel,
           wife              2, O, 1,
       DEZERBOIS, captain of a small
           vessel, wife      2, 1,
31-P. Rue d'Orleans ( Orleans Street)
       FONTAINE, tailor, wife       2,
       ROBERT GUITAIN, wife, child    3,
       JOSEPH, workman, wife, child   3,
       St. PAUL, workman, wife, child  3,
       HONORE LAMBERT, wife       2,

Note: The streets of New Orleans as above named were
not of necessity the same position wise as the streets
bearing the same name today. Maps of the period show
the bulk of the village between the river front and
present day Dauphine ( then called Conty), and between
present day Iberville ( then called Rue d'Anguin)
to present day Ursulines ( then called Rue d'Arcenal,
and on some maps, Rue st. Adrien.) As is shown in the
above census, some of these streets had few residents,
having just been laid out, and subject to future
expansion. Further information is available from the
booklet " The Vieux Carre, New Orleans, its Plan, its
Growth, its Architecture", by Samuel Wilson, Jr.
published by the Bureau of Governmental Research for
the City of New Orleans, December 1968.

\* \* \* \* \* \* \* \* \* \*

LIST OF THOSE PERSONS REQUESTING NEGROES
FROM THE COMPANY, DATED OCTOBER 1726.

BRUSLE, of New Orleans
BEAUPRE, indigo grower at Chapitoulas
MOUSSEL, indigo grower at Chapitoulas
ETIENNE ROY, of Petit Dezeri ( Little wilderness)
BREZILLIER, of Pascagoula
RICHAUME, of New Orleans
SOUBAGNIE of New Orleans
St. JULIEN, of Cannes Brulee ( Burnt Canes)
AUGUSTIN LANGLOIS of English Turn
La PRADE of English Turn
FRAPE of Tonica
DuPUY PLANCHARD, aide major
MIRAGOUIN of Mobile
RILIEUX of Pascagoula
SANSON of New Orleans
CHAPERON of English Turn
JOSEPH CARRIERE of English Turn
COUSTILLAS, officer
BONNAUD, storekeeper
DREUX brothers of New Orleans
De CHAVANNES, secretary to the council
TRONQUIDY
ROSSARD, clerk of the council
CABASSIER of English Turn
RENE CHESNEAU of Tincoas
HEMMERY of New Orleans
BELLEGARDE of New Orleans
POUPART of New Orleans
VERRET of Cannes Brulee ( Burn Canes)
CLAUDE BAILLY
JOSEPH BAILLY
De la BOUILLONNERIE of Natchez
LEONNARD of English Turn
VIGER of New Orleans
KESQUE of the German Village
YANS of the German Village
BUSSON, indigo grower
FUINKRERE
PLAISANCE
TRUDEAU of New Orleans
RAQUET of New Orleans
Concession of Ste. Reyne
Concession of De MEZIERES

MASSY of English Turn
POLOIN
DALCOURT of New Orleans
CHEVAL of New Orleans
BROSSET, surgeon
MANDEVILLE, Captain
DUVAL, auditor for the company
Le BORME, of Bayougoulas
PERRET of Bayougoulas
De NOYAN  of Cannes Bruslee
ETIENNE of New Orleans
St. MARTIN of New Orleans
BONNAVENTURE of Cannes Brulee
DARBY, director of concession of CANTILLON
BALCOURT of New Orleans
La RIVIERE of New Orleans
FLEURIEU of New Orleans
PELLERIN of Natchez
DARGARAY
Du QUENION
Des MONGE
CHENAL of Tincoas
Rev father BEAUBOIS of the Jesuits
Bishop SERRURIAN
La FRENIERE of Chapitoulas
De LERY of Chapitoulas
BEAULIEU of Chapitoulas
MARCHE de la TOUR
ETIENNE LANGLOIS of Bayouc
LOUIS LANGLOIS of New Orleans
De GAUVRET, officer
L'ARCHEVEQUE of New Orleans
JOSEPH LARCHEVEQUE of New Orleans
HUBERT of Chapitoulas
CHAMILLY of New Orleans
COUSSINE of New Orleans
JACQUES CARRIERE
FRANCOIS CARRIERE  ( mentioned together)
BALOY
Du.BREUIL of Chapitoulas
PROVENCHE of New Orleans
BUREAU of English Turn
GUICHARD of Cannes Bruslee
TIXERANT of Chouachas
CAZENBERGUE of New Orleans

B-26

BERGERON of New Orleans
RlVARD of Bayouc ( Bayou St. John)
DOLLY BONPART of Chaouachas
DANTIONNE of Petit Dezeri
De VILLAINVILLE, officer at Natchez
PICHON, auditor for M. De la CHAISE
PREVOST, bookkeeper
FRANCHOMME, officer at Illinois
La GOUBLAYE of New Orleans
PUJOS of Cannes Brulee
DONNE of Colas
HARACE cf Cannes Brulee
La COSTE of Colas
SERECHMAN   of New Orleans
DuBRET of New Orleans
La CANNUE of New Orleans
SCHMIT of New Orleans
La GRANGE of Grande Colas
La MAURY of Grande Colas
SUDRY of Cannes Brulee
MALATIER of Cannes Brulee
BRU, cashier for the Company
FILARS, former captain of the (ship) La Loire
Le PAGE of Natchez
DAUPHIN of Cannes Brulee
BOURBEAU of New Orleans
De MORAND, inspector of workmen
widow TRAPANIER of New Orleans
NEBOUT tobacco manufacturer
NICOLAS QUIDOR of Natchez
La SONDE, surgeon at Natchez
POMMIER of Colas
RENAUD of the concession of mines
POUDRET of Illinois
M. FLEURIAU, attorney general
Le HOUX of New Orleans
BARRIER of New Orleans
St. AMAND of New Orleans
LABRY of Colas
BERGUE, a german of New Orleans
FERRAND of Cannes Brulee
PREVOST, indigo grower
MORISSET, former commissary cashier
HUGUES MKEERT, english gaudronnier (?)
          of Mobile
HUET of Mobile

B-26

FONTAILLE of Mobile
PREVOST of Mobile
THOMAS ABELIANE of Mobile
PETIT of Mobile
LUSSER of Mobile
BENOIST, officer of Mobile
OLIVIER of Mobile
JACOBIN BELZAGUY of Mobile( Gaudronnier)
ARNAUD de LISLE of Isle Dauphine
La POINTE of Pascagoula
de la RIVIERE of Pascagoula ( mentioned
                           together)
LAVERGNE of Pascagoula
PIERRE RENAUD dit St. LAURENT
EDME BARON
CRELY

\* \* \* \* \* \* \* \* \* \*

NOTES ON THE CENSUS OF 1727

This census taken by order of Governor Perier does
not include the areas along the gulf coast ( Mobile
and Biloxi) , nor does it include Illinois and the
other smaller installations in Louisiana.

The totals for this census, which includes New Orleans
proper, the settlements along the Mississippi river
from its mouth to Pointe Coupee, and smaller areas
populated along Lake Ponchartrain, the Bayou St. John
and Gentilly ( Chantilly), are:

| | |
|---|---|
| French citizens ( Masters) | 1327 persons |
| Servants of european origin ( engagees) | 133 persons |
| Negro slaves | 1561 persons |
| Indian slaves | 75 persons |

These are numbered in the following pages in the right
hand columns by masters, servants, negro slaves, and
indian slaves. No number or a zero in a column indicates
no one in that household in that category.

The original of this census also shows the number of
cows, horses, and pigs.

This census is separated into two parts, the first
being New Orleans and environs, the second being those
householders along the river. In the last category,
especially on page B-27-5 and B-27-6 are the remnants
of the Germans who were settled along the left bank
of the river above New Orleans.  It is interesting to
compare this census with page A-26-3 and A-26-4 of the
census preceeding ( 1726) especially as to the French
attempt toward the spelling of German surnames. Many
of these entries are the same people but the different
census taker had different ideas toward the proper
spelling of these names.

As is the usual practice, transients such as soldiers
serving in the area for this period are not mentioned
although some former soldiers who settled are now
mentioned, and  when the soldiers brought their wives,
the wives are included in the census tables.

-27

CENSUS OF NEW ORLEANS AS
REPORTED BY M. PERIER, COMMANDANT GENERAL
OF LOUISIANA, JULY 1, 1727

1. Sur la place ( adjoining the "Place d'Armes")
   M. PERIER, commandant general,
                 his wife, M. de CHAMBELLAN,
                 the son of M. PERIER,
                 St. MOUDROLLOIS, secretary
                                       6, 4, 5, 0
2. A la direction ( the office of the management
                 of the colony)
   M. de la CHAISE, commissioner of
                 the king, his sons      2, 2, 3, 0
3. In the house belonging to the government
   M. de BOISBRIANT, lieutenant
   of the king for the province     1, 3, 1, 4
4. At the hospital on the Rue du Quay ( Levee street,
   now Decateur, along the river front)
                 Names of sick habitants
   JACQUES Le FEUVES, sailor
   child of JEAN VIEL
   GUILLAUME CHAMPION
   RENE Le JET, turner
   JARIA, blacksmith
   JEAN JOUANNE. carpenter
   PIERRE a german
   BALTAZARD, also a german
   JACQUES JENETEL, laborer
   RABOCK, swiss laborer
   JOSEPH LOUIS, workman
   JACQUES MOUSSET, indigo worker
   wife of RINGET, and 2 children
   wife of LOREN
   wife of La VIOLETTE
   wife of BOURDON, and her child
   wife of BALTAZARD, and her child
   wife of La PIERRE
   wife of St. JEAN
   widow La FOND
                 total at the hospital   25,
5. Rue du Quay, habitants along the river front
                 Le sieur DAMARON, druggist, wife  2, 0, 2, 1
                 Le sieur RAGUET, wife, 4 children 6, 0, 4,
                 BELLEVEUE, caretaker of the hospital,
                                 wife, child          3,
                                                   A-27

```
Le sieur DURIVAGE, contractor,
            wife, child                3, 3, 2, 1
Le sieur DUVAL, cashier, wife,
            child                      3, 0, 2, 1
Le sieur MAISONNEUVE, commissioner
            for Sieur DUVAL,           1,
Le sieur PREVOST, first bookeeper,
            BALLEY, second bookeeper   2,
Le sieur PELLERIN, warehouse guard,
            with Sieur MORISSET,
            employee                   2, 0, 2,
BLANPIN, washerwoman for the
            hospital                   1,
Le sieur CARITON, tailor,
            wife, child                3, 4,
ROY, blacksmith                        1,
ROGER                                  1,
LOUIS CHARTIER, his wife, a boy,
            a girl, a small boy,
            at the hospital            4,
MICHEL BORDIER, baker                  1, 2,
M. BONNAUD, former warehouse guard     1, 2, 1, 1
M. BROUTIN, engineer with
            GONINCHON                  2, 3, 2,
M. de NOYAN, wool comber?
            and his brother            2, 0, 9
JEAN GEORGES PICH, german brewer,
            wife, 2 children           4,
DAVID MUNIER, carpenter, wife          2,
ESTIENNE BOELLE, joiner                1,
NICOLAS ADAM, wig maker                1,
GILLES Le BRESSON                      1,
M. ADRIEN, carpenter                   1, 0, 3,
HONNORI ROTUREAU, miller               1,
JULIEN DORE, carpenter                 1,
```

6. Rue de Chartres ( Chartres street)

```
GAMBIE, carpenter, wife                2,
Du BOIS, carpenter                     1,
M. Le BLANC                            1, 0, 2, 1
M. MORAND, inspector of works,
            wife                       2, 0, 7,
M. de St. MARTIN                       1,
M. BIMONT, employee of the old
            management with M.
            BERNOUDAT                  2, 1,
```

JEAN JOST, a german, wife,
   small girl       3,
M. BRUSLE, councillor, wife, child 3, 0, 5,
M. de MANDEVILLE, major, wife,
   child        3, 0, 3,
M. PRAT, doctor and councillor  1,
BONNAVENTURE ROBERT, tailor, wife 2,
ANTOINE JACIR, a boy tailor   1,
Le sieur SARAZIN, wife, 3 children5, 0, 2,
Le sieur VALLERAN, dealer in poultry,
   wife, small girl    5, 1,
M. de la GARDE, director of the
   concession of M. CHAUMONT1,
CHARLES FRANCOIS Le MOINE, joiner,
   wife        2, 1,
TOINNETTE ZANBON PENIGAULT, child 2,
Le sieur DUBUISSON, employee of the
   council       1,
M. ROSSARD, notary in chief of the
   council of the king,
   commissioner DROY  2, 0, 2,
an indian slave belonging to
   M. RENAUD, captain  0, 0, 0, 1
Le sieur DECOUR, boy worker in the
   warehouse, and TESSON,
   his associate    2,
Le sieur CLAIRFONTAINE, employee
   of the warehouse   1,
ARNAUD RECHE dit BELAIR, his wife
   and 3 children    5,
JACQUES OZANNE, cooper   1,
SIMON Le MAIRE, cooper   1,
PIERRE PASSERAT, gardener for the
   company     1,
PIERRE THOMELIN, joiner, wife,
   2 children     4,
M. BRUSLE, habitant,  wife  4, 0, 1
7. Rue de Conde (  now continuation of Chartres)
   Father RAPHAEL, grand master of
     the priest of New Orleans,
     and brother priests 3, 1, 1, 1
THOMAS ASSELIN, wife, child  3,
MARIE FASARD, widow, child   2,
M. de LASSUS, engineer    1, 2,
JEAN CARON, baker, wife    2, 1,
JEAN BAPTISTE CHERNIER,
   dit PROVENCAL    1,

St. LUCE, a german                        1,
TOUSSAINT PÉRAUT, carpenter               1,
JOSEPH MOREAU, locksmith,
        3 children                      4,
ANTOINE MALOT, tailor, wife               2,
POUYADON, surgeon                         1,
CLAUDE HEU, coppersmith                   1,
ANDRE VILLEUX                             1,
JEAN BAPTISTE PROVENCHI, wife        2, 0, 1,
CLAUDE IMBERT, fisherman, wife,
        child                           3,
BARBE CHEVALIER                           1,
Madam TRUDEAU, 4 children            5, 1, 4,
JEAN VUIME dit CHARPENTRAS,
        wife, child                     3,
MARIE MAGDELAINE DOYART, wife of
        RENE MALAIN dit SANS
        CHAGRIN                         1,
MERANGUIER                                1,
PIERRE ROBERT, joiner                     1,

8. Rue Royal ( Royal street)
FRANCOIS MUGUET                           1,
MARIE LOUISE BRETON, widow,
        2 children                      3,
JEAN TULIPE, former soldier
        from Mobile                     1,
ALBERT FONDELET, german laborer,
        2 children                      3,
MARIE TOURNELOTTE, widow with
        2 children                      3,
GRANDJEAN, of the distribution            1,
MARIE CHEVALIER, wife of sieur
        GRAU, accountant of the
        hospital                        1,
CLAUDE GOURMET dit CONTOIS,
        commissioner of the fort,
        wife, child                     3,
NICOLAS PICHON, candle maker,
        wife, 2 children                4,
ANTOINE BARTHELEMY dit La GARENNE
        with BOESMIEN, a child,
        and orphan boy                  3,
HILAIRE CHESNAU, gunner,
        2 children                      3,
ANTOINE MICOU, carpenter                  1,
MICHAU, day laborer                       1,

```
SIMON ABUCOIN, carpenter            1,
FRANÇOISE Le FEUVRE, widow , with
          Sieur BONNAVENTURE,
          3 children               4, 1, 2,
BLANVILAIN, day worker              1,
AUBERT, wife, child                 3,
CHARLES GONOIN                      1,
GRESLIN, formerly of the concession
          Of M. LAW                 1,
JOSEPH PETIT, roofer, wife,
          2 children               4, 0, 1,
LIVIEN POIRIER, gunsmith, wife,
          child                     3,
FRANÇOIS Le BOULAIR dit SANS REGRET,
          wife, child, orphan boy  4,
FRANCOIS ORSE, tailor               1,
CLAUDE FRANÇOIS MARIN, tailor       1,
the wife of MONDAUBAN, soldier,
          child                     2,
GUILLAUME Le MOIRE, patron, wife,
          child                     3,
ANTOINE La RIVIERE, sailor,
          now at Mobile            (1)*
PIERRE PITARD dit La FRANCE,
          wife, child               3,
PIERRE Le MARCHAND dit BRINVILLE   1,
JEAN MANSIEN, patron, wife,
          2 children               4,
JACQUES POUILLARD, traveller        1,
JACQUES FRANCOIS JACQUET, wife,
          2 children               4,
JACQUES CHENIER, canadian with
          ISABELLE LUCE, his wife,
          a small boy               3,
JEAN L'HOPITAL, sailor             (1)*
JACQUES Le MAIRE                   (1)*
FRANÇOIS LIMESLE, baker            1, 0, 2,
widow SAUCIER, 4 children          5, 0, 3,
CLAUDE FONTAINE, traveller, wife,
          2 children               4, 1,
ROCH MICHEL, employee of the
          council, wife, 4 children 5, 0, 1,
JULIEN BINARD, master tailor,
          wife, child               3,
```

\* Not counted in this place

A-27

```
GUILLAUME PERRIER, commander of
        the habitation of the
        company, wife,
        with 2 children              4,
JEAN L'EVESQUE                       1,
ANTOINE AUFRERE, wife, child         3,
GUILLAUME BOUSQUERAT, traveller      1,
SERVAY, employee , wife, child       1,
ANTOINE JOBELIN dit SANS SOUCY
        traveller, wife              2,
PIERRE CAILOU, mason, wife, child    3,
NICOLAS PIERROT dit VENDOME          1,
ANTOINE LEVENNE, wife, child         3,  0, 0, 2
MARIANNE PINVILLE, wife of BREDA,
        a soldier                    1,
LOUIS JARRY, innkeeper, wife, with
        JEAN BAPTISTE JARRY,
        his brother, child           5,
La JOYE, employee of La CAISSE       1,
CHARLES ROGER, employee              1,
JEAN BAPTISTE BEAUPRE                1,
a negro domestic of M. De MOUY       0, 0, 1,
M. FAZENDE, wife, M. de MOLIES,
        his mother, child            4, 0, 2,
CLAUDE HERPIN, merchant              1,
FLORENT DANVILLE, employee,
        wife, 2 children             4, 0, 2,
M. DUPUY PLANCHARD, officer, wife,
        M. DUPUY, his son            3, 0, 2,
a  negro belonging to
        M. de MERVEILLEUX            0, 0, 1,
JACQUES VINCENT, sheriff of the
        council, wife                2,
M. DUMANOIR, with Sieur LANGLOIS,
        employees of M. de la
        LIVAUDAIS                    3, 0, 1, 2
M. ESTIENNE, employee               1,
M. PERILLAUT, employee              1,
M. PAQUIER                          1,
```

9. Rue de Bourbon ( Bourbon street)

```
PAUL Le BLEU, wife, child            3,
GRATIEN l'ANTIC, workman, wife,
        3 children                   5,
FRANCOIS VITREQUIN dit COUILLARD,
        of Natchez, 2 children       3,
```

```
PIERRE PICQUERIE, baker, wife,
          2 children                    4, 1,
JACQUES SAUNIER, blacksmith             1,
M. de TRONQUIDY, captain of the
          vessel La Loire, wife,
          2 children                    4,
ANTOINE PATIN, carpenter, wife,
          4 children                    6,
BAPTISTE FONTAINE, apprentice
          carpenter                     1,
ANDRE BERTRAND, carpenter, wife,
          4 children                    2, 1,
CATHERINE ONDAR, wife of dec.
          BEAULIEU, sergeant            1,
CLAUDE DORMOIS, day workman,
          wife, 2 children              4,
FRANCOIS MANSIAN, joiner, wife,
          2 children of M. PHILIDON     2,
LOUIS PHILIDON, carpenter, wife,
          2 children not living
          at his residence              4,
FRANCOIS La CLAYE, major of the
          company, wife                 1,
CHRISTINE La VALLE, widow              1,
FRANCOIS CALLAIR, carpenter, wife       2,
FRANCOIS ALIX dit La ROSE, wife,
          coppersmith, and
          RENAUDE GERNAY,and an
          orphan girl                   3,
PHILIPES Le DUC, locksmith, wife        2,
ESTIENNE POULIN, day workman,
          wife                          2,
PIERRE FERAND, trader with the
          Houmas ( indian tribe)        1,
the wife of GAUTIER, a soldier          1,
CHRISTOPHE THOMAS, workman              1,
EVRARD, carpenter                       1,
JEAN RONDEAU, carpenter, wife           1,
DANIEL RAFLAND, roofer, wife,
          2 children                    4,
ANTOINE NOGRIEN, wife                   2,
BABAS, a currier ( Leather maker)       1,
AUJIBEAU, locksmith                     1,
MICHEL BROSSET, surgeon                 1,
JACAUES COQUELIN, wife, child           3,
```

A-27

FRANCOIS FROUTIER, locksmith,
        wife, child           3,
L'ANGLOIS, locksmith for the
        company,           1,
NICOLAS DARTEL, hunter, wife    2,
JACQUES DUPRE, joiner, wife, child3,
the wife of BERNARD, a soldier  1,
JOSEPH CARDON, laborer, wife    2,
PIERRE LEQUESNE, roofer       1,
MARIE GENEVIEVE GARNIER, wife of
        SANNUE, child        2,
St. QUENTIN, of Natchez       1,
JOSEPH MARIE, employee of a
        fisherman          2,
JEAN FRANCOIS BOURDON, carpenter,
        wife, 3 children     5,
ANTOINE BUREL, wife, child     3,
NICOLAS BRANTANT, gunsmith     1,
LION, maker of nails         1,
GUPAYEL, maker of nails       1,
MONSIGNAC dit PIPIC, traveller  1,
JEAN BLOQUIN, engagee      0, 1,
MICHEL CARON, patron, wife     2,
La ROCHE, carpenter         1,
GASPARD DIDIER, joiner, wife,
        child             4,
Le sieur DUTOUR, employee     1,
BUSEAU                 1,
JEAN BAPTISTE BORE, wife      2,
CHARLES VINCENT, sailor      1,
ANNE MARGUERITTE, wife of
        CHARLES VINCENT     1,
the wife of BAGUETTE        1,
10. On the street crossing behind Bourbon ( This
   street was unnamed in 1727, but is now
Dauphine street).
        PIERRE BAUDOUIN, day worker,
                wife, child      3,
        FRANCOIS HUPE, former sailor,
                wife, child      3,
        BOUCHER, a boy carter     1,
        GILBERT BARIE, sailor for the
                company, wife, 2 children4,
        CHARLES DUPUIS dit ORLEANS,
                carter and hunter of the
                post at Akansas     1,

A-27

                    GUILLAUME FOUCHER, maker of nails,
                         wife, child                3,
                    PIERRE Le CLERC, shaper of wood,
                         wife, child                2,
                    JEAN SERPILLON, wife            2,
11. On the road to the bayou ( St. John), this
    city street is now called Grand Route St. John
    and was the portage of the indians between Lake
    Ponchartrain and the Mississippi river.
                    NICOLAS MARCHAND, patron, wife   2, 1,
                    MARTIN La FONTAINE, sailor        1,
                    JACQUES SILARD, traveller         1,
                    GENTILHOMME, patron of CANOT,
                         wife, child                 3,
                    PIERRE CONTOIS, wife, 2 children  4, 0, 1,
                    ANTOINE MEGNEUX, nail maker       1,
12. Rue de Conty ( Conti street)
                    M. de CHAVANNES, secretary to the
                         council                     1, 0, 2,
                    M. FLEURIAU, attorney general,
                         wife                        2, 0, 8,
                    M. MANADE, surgeon, wife          2,
                    M. GENOT                          1,
                    ANTOINE SET, german, wife,
                         2 children                   4,
                    MAGDELAINE BOULANGER, wife of
                         VAUVRAY, child               2,
                    FRANÇOIS GAGNEUR, fisherman, wife,
                         child                        3,
                    YSABELLE THULIE, wife of BONPART,
                         and THERESE, an orphan
                         domestic                    1, 1,
                    La BOURGEOIS, wife of DELAURIERS  1,
                    REINE                            1,
                    M. ALEXANDRE, surgeon, wife and
                         JOSEPH CASSARD              3, 1, 3,
                    SEBASTIEN ROBIDOU, master builder 1,
                    MAGDELAINE JAUVBEN               1,
                    SOISSONS, joiner, child          2,
                    BAPTISTE LOTTIER of Natchez      1,
                    MARTIN                           1,
                    BAYOU, of Natchez, and a child   2,
                    MAURICE COUNME, german, wife     2,
                    NICOLAS CHRISTIAN, wife          2,

                                        A-27

13. Rue St. Louis ( St. Louis street)
      Le sieur DUPLESSY               1,
      Les sieurs CORRANT, St. MARIE,
          and PITACHE             3,
      JEAN FRANCOIS St. AMAND, wife,
          2 children            4, 0, 0, 1
      IGNACE JET, joiner, wife      2,
      MARIE MAGDELAINE BACHELET, widow  1,
      ANTOINE JOSEPH de LATTES, joiner,  1,
      the wife of LAMBERT. a soldier    1,
      THERESE PECHOT              1,
      GILLES AVOT, blacksmith,
          wife, child            3,
      FRANCOIS SAUNIER, sailor    (1)*
14. Rue de Thoulouze (sic.) ( Toulouse street)
      FRANCOIS DIZIER, ironworker, wife 2,
      CLAUDE CHAPE              1,
      BARBE                   1,
      LOUIS DUGUE, surgeon, wife,
          2 children            4, 0, 1,
      La GOUBLAYE, employee of the
          warehouse, wife,
          2 children            4,
      ESTIENNE FILASSIER, orphan    1,
      NICOLAS CORDON, wood cutter   1,
      JEAN VINANTE, fisherman      1,
      NICOLAS MARTIN DUCHATEAU,
          shoemaker             1,
      PIERRE CARNET, sieur de LONG,
          wife, child             3,
      TOUSSAINT BOURELLIEN, carpenter
          for M. La LOIRE         1,
      FRANCOIS BRUNET, blacksmith   1,
      PIERRE LOT, carpenter of Natchez 1,
      MICHEL DAVRIL            1,
      MARIANNE CARIE           1,
      JEAN DUMAS              1,
      CLAUDINE JOUISON, wife of a
          soldier              1,
15. Rue st. Pierre ( St. Peter street)
      FRANCOIS GELARD, wife, 5 children 7, 0, 1,
      NICOLAS HUMBERT, blacksmith,
          wife, child             3,
      MARIANNE La FORGE, child    2,
      THERESE VALENVINNE, child   2,

ANDRE ROCHER, traveller from
            Illinois, wife           2,
MATHURIN SEIMARD, sailor        1,
AIME VIGNARD, wife             2,
FRANCOIS POTIER, sailor         1,
PIERRE RAGUETTE                1,
NICOLAS PROUET, carter, wife,
            child               3,
BARBIER, a german of the Tonicas
            Indian tribe, 2 children 3,
YVES PINET, gunsmith, his brother 2,
wife of JACQUES JOU, soldier,
            with her sister       2,
wife of JEAN ROBERT, soldier,
            3 children           4,
ANDRE CONARD, carter, wife,
            2 children           4,
MATHURIN MENEROLLE, locksmith,
            wife                2,
PIERRE Le COMTE, carter       1,
wife of JEAN METAYER dit La
            RIVIERE, corporal     1,
JEAN AUDIN dit La FONTAIN    1,
MARIE LARZILLJERS, wife of
            CARDON, child        2,
JEAN VAQUIER, workman        1,
VIVIEN BAILLY, sailmaker, wife,
            child               3,
M. SENET, captain of the port,
            his son            2,

16. Rue d'Orleans ( Orleans street)
    PIERRE GARGARET, messenger for the
            council, his wife, child 3,
FRANCOIS JOUTEUR, wife, child   3,
PIERRE MARTINOT BEDOT, wife, child3,
JEAN LEGER, joiner           1,
wife of BELAIR, soldier     1,
JEAN VARREUIL, gunsmith     1,
JOSEPH AMELOT, fisherman, child  2,
JACQUES CANTEREL, child      2,
FRANCOISE CAFFE, widow of SAMSON,
            child               2,
JEAN LOUIS, patron of CANOT    1,
ANTOINE GOFFION, day workman   1,
FRANCOIS FONDEN, wife, sister   3, 1,

A-27

```
M. BION, employee                    1,
HONNORE, foreman                     1,
LAMBERT, foreman, wife, child        3,
PIERRE TYET, turner                  1,
PIERRE FRANCOIS FONTAIN, tailor,
        wife                         2,
PIERRE La HOUX, of Akansas, wife,
        child                        3,
wife of NICOLAS BOUCHE, habitant of
        Yasou, 2 children           3,
ANDRE COURSAN, butcher, wife,
        3 children                   5,
LOUIS LEDAIN, tailor                 1,
ANDRE COURSAN, hairdresser ?
        child                        2,
M. d'AUSSEVILLE, councillor of the
        superior council      1, 0, 3,
ROBERT GUILLAIN, shoemaker, wife,
        child                        3,
NICOLAS NOISET, wife, child          3,
```
17. Rue st. Anne ( St. Anne street)
```
CHRISTINE BLARD, wife of JEAN
        LABI, 2 children             4,
PIERRE JOSEPH de l'ISLE dit DUPART,
        wife, child                  3,
JOSEPH LAZOU, captain of a boat,
        wife                  2, 0, 1,
CHARLES DURAND dit La JUILLADE,
        captain of a boat            1,
FRANCOIS DEJERBOIS                   1,
the wife of FRANCOIS HERISE,
        soldier, 2 children          3,
ANTOINE LONI, tailor, wife, child 3, 1,
LOUIS PERON, sailor, wife         1, 1,
JEANDRAU, sailor                     1,
GUILLAUME VIVIEN, sailor             1,
MARLESGOF, sailor                    1,
JEAN MELAIN dit DORANGE, blacksmith,
        wife                         2,
the wife of CLAUDE MAIRAIN,
        soldier                      1,
ALAIN JARDELA, charcoal maker,
        wife, child                  3,
PIERRE CLERAU, blacksmith            1,
DANIEL, maker of nails               1,
```

```
                CLAUDE BEDESON, blacksmith,
                        his negro              1, 0, 1,
                La GONSALEAU, wife of a soldier
                        of Mobile              1,
                The wife of COURTABLEAU, who
                        deserted , child       2,
                NICOLAS TOUZE dit RICHARD, sailor(1)*
                JULIEN GAUTIER, sailor of Mobile (1)*
18, Rue Dumaine ( Dumaine street)
                M. MUNNIER, a canadian, with
                        GUYON, a canadian      2, 0, 3,
                ISABELLE BERLIN, wife of JEAN
                        PASCAL, child          2,
                JEAN BIGUARD , turner, wife,
                        child                  3,
                CLAUDE CHARLES, tailor         1,
                wife of JEAN JELIZOTOUIA, who
                        left for France        1,
                ESTIENNE BARRATON,carter, wife,
                        who is a neice of
                        de CHERMONT, child     2, 1,
                JEAN NAVES, day workman         1,
19. Rue de Clairemont ( Clairmont street. This street
    is now called St. Philip street)
                JACQUES VEILLON, turner        1,
                La DUSABON, of Illinois        1,
                JEAN PHILIPE La PRARIE, wife    2,
                wife of JEAN de FREDERICH dit
                        La FONTAIN, tanner?     1,
                FRANCOISE MUGUET               1,
                ALBERT FONDELIEK, german laborer,
                        wife, 2 children       4,
                MARIE LOUISE BRETON, widow with
                        2 children             3,
                MARIE TOURNELOTTE, widow with
                        2 children             3,
                GRANDJEAN of the distribution  1,
                MARIE CHEVALIER, wife of M. GRAU,
                        aid at the hospital    1,
                CLAUDE GOURET ditCONTOIS, commander
                        of fortifications,
                        wife, 2 children       4,
                NICOLAS PECHON, chevalier,
                        wife, 2 children       4,
                ANTOINE BERTHELEMY dit La GARENNE,
                        planter, 2 children,
                        and an orphan boy      3,
                                               A-27
```

```
       HILAIRE CHESNAU, gunner, child      2,
       MICHAUX, day workman                1,
       SIMON ABINION, carpenter            1,
       FRANCOISE Le FEVRES, widow with
               3 children                  4, 1, 2,
       LOUIS BROUET, wheelwright, child    2,
       MARIE Le MOINE, wife of CHARLES
               MERCIER dit SANS CHAGRIN,
               child                       2,
       wife of La VIOLLETTE, child         2,
       NICOLAS GUIDCU, sailor, wife,
               child                       2, 1,
       Le sieur BERNOUDY, employee         1,
       THERESE MARIE, orphan girl          1,
       wife of COLLER dit JOLYCOEUR
               sergeant, 2 children        3,
```

20. Habitants along the road to the bayou and to
    Chantilly ( now called Gentilly).

```
       GODET, wife                         2,
       LOUIS CONGO, M. de SHAUTES,
               workmen, wives, both
               negroes                     0, 0, 2,
       M. and Madame de GAUVRIT, captain
               of the Infantry,
               3 children                  5, 0, 5,
       LANGLOIS, wife, 3 children          5, 0, 7,
       JOSEPH, wife, 4 children            5, 0,15, 2
       M. and Madam RIVARD, 5 children     7, 0,22,
       FRANCOIS                            1, 1, 5,
       RIVIT, habitant of Chantilly,
               wife, 2 children            4,
       M. LAUBAINNIER, wife, 2 children    4, 1, 5,
       The brothers DREUX                  2, 1,12, 2
       JEAN CAZIMBERT, german, his wife,
               and his son                 3,
       another german habitant, wife, son  3,
```

21. Habitants of La Balise ( The fort at the mouth of
    the Mississippi river)

```
       M. DUVERGIER, commandant            1,
       Le R. P. GASPARD, capuchin priest   1,
       St. MICHEL, warehouse guard         1.
       BELDIE, surgeon                     1,
       M. FRANCOIS, first pilot,  wife,
               2 children                  4,
       PIERRE TRIET, second pilot, wife    2.
```

A-27

```
              M. PINOULT, workman               1,
              MATHURIN Le BAS, carpenter        1,
              RESIN DELAURIE, carpenter         1,
              FRANCOIS LIGUY  woodcutter        1,
              JEAN BUREAU, woodcutter           1,
              JOSEPH GAY dit DAUPHINE,
                        woodcutter              1,
              VINCENT BAUGNEMONT, woodcutter    1,
              PAUL VITRE, woodcutter, wife      2,
              JACOB VISCERENNE, woodcutter      1,
              JACAUES ROZIER, woodcutter        1,
              TOUSSAINT PERAULT, woodcutter     1,
              ESTIENNE GIRAULT, child           2,
              JACQUES SAUTIER, joiner           1,
              HEU, joiner                       1,
              JACAUES DUBOIS, locksmith         1,
              negroes of the port belonging to
                        the company          0, 0,55,
```
22. Habitants on the shore of Lake Ponchartrain,
    on the north side
```
              Le sieur DUSCHESNE, with ANION   2, 2,11,
              La COMBE                         1, 0, 1,
              La CROIX                         1, 0, 1,
              BARIE                            1,
              JEAN VIS, and his son            2,
```
23. Habitants 4 leagues to the west of New Orleans
    along the Bayou des Tendupar ( Bayou La Fourche?)
```
              THOMAS                        1, 0, 3, 1
              La SALLE                      1, 0, 5,
```

            *  *  *  *  *  *  *  *  *  *

CONTINUATION OF THE CENSUS OF M.
PERIER REPORTED JULY 1, 1727. HABITANTS IN
THE ENVIRONS OF NEW ORLEANS, ALONG THE RIVER

I. RIGHT BANK ASCENDING

```
GABRIEL MESTAIN, wife, associate    3,
ALEXIS LE CORE                      1,
DRAPEAU, wife, 3 children           5, 0, 1,
Le sieur BUISSON, indigo grower     1, 0, 5,
DESLAIR, canadian, wife, sons       4, 0, 9,
Le sieur ARNAUD, canadian           1, 0, 4,
Le sieur CARRIERE, canadian, wife,
            child                   3, 0, 7,
FRANCOIS CARRIERE, canadian, wife,
            2 children              4, 0,31, 6
JOSEPH CARRIERE, canadian, wife,
            2 children              4, 1,14, 1
Le sieur TIXERANT, wife,
            5 children              7, 1,45, 7
BOSER                               1, 0, 1, 2
Le sieur CHENAT, with
            FRANCOIS PERABE         2, 0, 2, 1
JOSEPH FAGUET                       1, 0, 1,
PIERRE FILLARD                      1, 0, 1,
ANTOINE BRUSLE                      1, 0, 7,
JEAN BAPTISTE LEONARD, 2 sons       3, 0, 2,
Le sieur CHAMILLY                   1, 0, 4, 2,
PIERRE MANADE, wife                 2, 0, 8,
Le sieur CLAUDE JOUSSET, wife,
            child                   3, 1, 7, 2
JOSEPH CHAPERON, wife, an orphan
            boy                     3, 0, 7,
FRANCOIS LARCHE, occupying the
            habitation of De ROCHES 1, 0, 3,
HENRY FLAMAND, age 45, wife, child  3, 0, 1,
BERTRAND JAFFRE dit La LIBERTE,
            wife                    2, 0, 7, 2
JACQUES CHARPENTIER occupying the
            habitation of Le sieur
            St. MARTIN as director  1, 0,14,
Le sieur de la GARDE, director for
            M. de CHAUMONT          1, 3,17,
M. de MANDEVILLE, wife, occupants   2, 0, 9,
M. JACQUES PREVOST, commander,and
            for M. RAGUET           0, 1,20,
```

B-27

Le sieur MAREST de la TOUR,
        ensign, and his brother  2, 0, 9, 1
Le sieur DALCOURT, wife, 2
        children              4, 0,25,
for M. TRUDEAU            1, 0,45,
For le sieur DUPUY PLANCHARD,
        ensign            0, 0, 8,
Le sieur de la BOULAYE, wife    2, 0, 8.
Le sieur COUSTILLAS, lieutenant with
Le sieur des CAYRAC        2, 0,33, 2
for le sieur CANTILLU, director
        Le sieur DALBY      1, 2,12,
The brewery of the DREUX brothers
        occupants, cousins of
        M. DRILLANT, and daughter
                        3, 0, 5, 2
The reverend priest Jesuit, father
        BEAUBOIS, brothers of the
        order, Le sieur BORE,
        M. and Madame VAUPARIS  7, 1,13,
for le sieur BONNANT, occupant
        JEAN DESLAU        1, 0, 6,
BERGERON, wife, child      3, 0, 2,
JACQUES OUBES, wife, sons    3,
ANDRE FRESCHEMENT, wife,
        2 children           4, 0, 1, 2
M. BELAIR               1, 0, 5, 1
Le sieur Le ROY, wife      2, 0, 8,
for SIMON CONIBE, german, wife  2,
for DANIEL PORAGE, wife, child  3,
for JEAN DENALISE, his wife, and
        CHETIPENE         3,
FRANCOIS DESUE, wife, child,
        and associate       4,
AUGUSTIN GOUY, wife        2,
M. DUBREUIL of Chapitoulas, his wife,
        2 children, and
        sieur LAUTHEAUME    3, 0,45, 1
M. DELERY, his wife, 4 children,
        MOREAU, and DECOLE   7, 0,59, 1
M. de BEAULIEU, wife, child   3, 2,52, 5
Le sieur CHAUVIN de la FRENIERE,
        wife, 3 children, and
        Le sieur HUGAUT     6, 1,87, 6

```
M. KOLLY, M. and Madame LEMAIRE,
        Le sieur DUBERVE and
        Le sieur QUIMPER              5, 1,73,
JOSEPH VERET, wife, child             3, 0, 1,
CHARLES BON, sergeant, dit
        LANGEVIN, wife,
        2 children                    4,
for M. BENAC, at another habitation
For M. DIRON, Le sieur De NOYON
        occupant                      1, 0,43,
M. BENAC                              1, 1, 31
FRANCOIS DAUPHIN, wife, 2 children    2, 1,
JOSEPH DAUPHIN, wife                  2,
ANDRE CREPE, wife, child              3, 0, 2,
DENIS FERANDON, wife                  2, 1,
JEAN de SUDRY, wife                   2,
FRANCOIS CHEVAL, wife, 4 children     4, 0, 3,
ANTOINE Le BORNE, wife, child         3, 1,
RENE DENAIRIN, and his brother        2,
DEPOUCHE dit La CHAPELLE, wife        2,
HENRY AUTIEN, widower                 1, 1,
LOUIS ROUSSEAU dit LA FLAMME,
        wife, and associate           3,
JOSEPH QUINTRE, wife, 2 children      4, 0, 2,
FRANCOIS ROBERT                       1,
FRANCOIS PHILIPE DUMIE, wife,
        child                         3,
BELANDEAU, wife, child                3, 1, 1,
La COSTE, wife, 2 children            3,
LAUMIER, wife, 2 children             4,
FRANCOIS COLLIN, wife                 2, 0, 1, 1
JEAN BARBOT, wife, child              3, 0, 2,
JEAN PERET, wife, 2 children          4,
GILBERT DUMAS                         1,
PIERRE BARON, wife                    2, 0, 5,
SEBASTIEN BONNET, wife, 2 children    4,
DAVOERT LEGROS, wife, 2 children      4,
DALBERT Le CUIR, and his son          2, 0, 2,
```

The above represents 83 individual land assignments along the right bank of the Mississippi river, in the order named.

II. LEFT BANK ASCENDING

```
            Le sieur ROQUIGNY, manager of
                   concession of LE BLANC      1, 1,25,
            Le sieur BOURBEAU, farmer,
                   habitation of the conce-
                   ssion of St, Catherine
                   at Chaouachas               1, 1,17,
            Le sieur LABRO, wife, 3 children   5, 0,22, 2
       M. MARCILLY, mason, wife, with
                   Le sieur TREPANIER,
                   the wife of VAUBERCY,
                   Madame TREPANIER, made-
                   moiselle FRANCOISE TREPANIER,
                   with 2 other children, of
                   M. TREPANIER's nephew       7, 1,20, 1
            Le sieur BIGOT, canadian           1, 0, 2,
       COUSSINNE, wife, 3 children             5,
       PEAUL BARRE, canadian, wife             2, 0, 3, 1
            Le sieur MASSY, an orphan boy      2, 0,27,
       M. FAZENDE, with M. MORIERE as
                   occupant                    1, 1, 4,
            Le sieur ALBERT BONNE, canadian,
                   wife, 3 children            5, 0, 9,
       HENRY BUQUOIS, wife, child              3, 0, 4,
       JEAN BAPTISTE BOURBEAU, wife            2, 9, 6,
       LOUIS LANGLOIS, canadian                1, 0, 2,
       CLAUDE FLEURIE, with ANNE FLEURIE
                   his wife. 2 children        4,
       JEAN PIERRE EMERY dit La SONDE,
                   wife, 2 children            4,
       AUGUSTIN LANGLOIS, wife, child          3, 0, 3,
       M. PROVENCHE, wife, and LA VIVE,
                   an orphan                   2, 0, 3.
       for M. de BIENVILLE, occupant
                   FRANCOIS CARDINAL,
                   M. de NOYAN brothers
                   living there                1, 1,65,
                   other negroes for NOYAN     0, 0, 7,
       GEORGES RESQUENET, a german,
                   wife, 2 children            4, 0, 2,
       habitation belonging to the company,
                   M. CHARNEY, occupant        1, 0,79,
       for M. PERIER, commandant,
                   Le sieur ARNELIN,
                   occupant                    1, 0,28,
```

B-27

```
JACQUES LARCHE LAINE, age 29,
          wife, 3 children          5, 0, 6,
JOSEPH LARCHE                        1, 0, 2,
Le sieur VIGE, wife, child          3, 1, 8,
Madame RICHAUME, widow with
          4 children                5, 1, 5,
Le sieur DAIGLE dit MABOROUG,
          wife, child               3,
JEAN CURVERA, wife                  2,
M. de BELISLE, officer              1,
M. MICHEL, wife, child              3, 3, 5,
M. PETIT de CONTANGE, with
          his brother               2,
M. PETIT de LIVILLIERS, officers
          of the company, wife,
          brother, and M. de VERTEUIL
                                    3, 2, 9,
CLAUDE BAILLIFS, wife, child        3,
LAURENT QUAY, wife                  2,
THOMAS GUICHARD, wife               2,
JEAN VEUFS, wife, child             3, 0, 1,
ANTOINE KOUR with LOUIS LIMAILLIS   2,
M. St. JULIEN                       1, 1,18,
PIERRE SERRILLE, wife, child, and
          brother and his wife      4,
GERMAIN VAUDRAY, wife, sister       3,
JEAN PAGE de LERAS, wife            2, 0, 2,
KIMON of the house of PETIT         1,
JEAN LABI, wife, with MOREAU        2, 1,
SAINTON, wife, 3 children           5, 0, 1,
JACQUES ROBLA, wife, 3 children     5,
JEAN VILLIER dit LIONNOIS, wife     2,
JEAN ADAM  CALLEMAR, wife,
          3 children                5,
DANSIER PAU, wife                   2,
d'OLLEPHON, wife, 2 children        3,
PHILIPPE CHAUME, widower, child     2,
ANDRE ARMANT, wife, 2 children      4,
CRISTIAN CERVE, wife, child         3,
MARGUERITTE BEAUMON , widow
          child                     2,
PIERRE BENARD, wife, 2 children     4,
ANDRE CANAN, child                  2,
BAPTISTE FREDERIC, wife,
          3 children                5, 2,
```

```
JOSEPH VACHEBA, wife, child          3,
VALERIEN CAYON, wife, child          3,
JEAN JARRY, wife, child              3,
ANDRE STUNGUE, wife, child, and
          an old lady               4,
JEAN PIERRE MANGAGE, wife, child     3,
FREDERIC  MARQUELES, wife age 28     2,
JEAN  YRESMEN, wife, 3 children      5,
MARQUE SCELLER, wife                 2,
ADAM SCHMITTE, widower , child       2,
ANDRE TRAIGUE, wife, 3 children      5,
M. DARENSBOURG, former captain
          of the Germans            1,
JEAN ANDRE SMITE, wife,
          2 children               4,
MICHEL OUN, wife, child             3,
FRANCOIS KINGLE, wife, 2 children   4,
BASTIEN JENGUE, wife, 2 children    4,
MICHEL FUGUE, wife, 2 children      4,
JACQUES CORIDE, wife                2,
GASPARD TOUPSE, wife, 2 children    4,
ADAM MADERNE, wife, 2 children      4, 2,
AMBROIZE AIDET, wife, child         3, 2,
LEONARD MAETOFF, wife, child        3,
ESTIENNE KESTIMA, wife, child       3,
BALTASAR MARIX, wife                2,
ANDRE SENSE, wife, 2 children       4,
WILLEIHME  SIRIAC, wife, child      3,
MARIE MAGDELAINE STERGE and her
          son                       2,
PIERRE SAINARIE, wife               2,
GEORGE TROCHER, wife                2,
BENARD DIVES, wife, 3 children      5,
JEAN CONERA FREDERIC, wife,
          4 children               6,
SIMON LEMBERT, wife, child         3,
JEAN ROMAIN, wife, child           3,
MARTIN LAMPARD, wife               2,
BERNARD ROCHE, wife, child         3,
JEAN COLLIN, wife, child, and
          an old woman             4,
JOSEPH CARTAN dit THOULOUZE,
          wife, 2 children         4,
M. DUBUISSON, director of the
          concession of BUISSONS   1, 4,72, 1
```

```
        de la Pointe Coupee,
        PIERRE  LA PORCHE, and his
                brother, habitants       2,
        PHILIPPE HAINAUD                 1,
        JEAN ALARD                       1,
        JOACHIM HAUSSY, wife             2,  0, 1,
        JACQUES, PALLIAR                 1,  0, 2,
        ANTOINE ANOTRAN, wife            2,
        FRANCOIS Le CUIR                 1,
        VALENTIN DAUBLIN, wife           2,
        JEAN FRANCOIS ALLAIN             1,
        ALEXANDRE BIENVENU               1,
        JACAUES DEVU, wife, 2 children   4,
        ANSEHNES FOUCAULT, wife, child   3,
        BERTHELMY MADRE, wife, child     3,
        LOUIS HOMARD                     1,
        LOUIS BAUDOIN, wife              2,
        JACQUES MOUSSET                  1,
        RENE GENOUY                      1,
```

The above represents 111 individual land assignments
along the left bank of  the Mississippi river, in
the order named, and includes the "german coast"
north of New Orleans and on the west bank of the
river.

\*   \*   \*   \*   \*   \*   \*   \*   \*   \*

LIST OF PERSONS MASSACRED AT NATCHEZ
NOVEMBER 28, 1729, AS REPORTED BY R.P. PHILIBERT,
CAPUCHIN PRIEST AND CERTIFIED JUNE 9, 1730.

de CHEPART, commandant
MASSE, lieutenant, wife and neice
DESNOYERS, 2nd lieutenant, and director of the
          concession at Terre Blanc, and
          commander of the fort
24 unnamed soldiers of the garrison
one named BELAIR escaped
BAILLY, director
La SONDE, surgeon major
LAURENT HURLOT, assistant surgeon
KNEPER, notary
FRANCOIS DUBREY, sacristan
DES LONGRAIS, director of the concession at
          St. Catherine
La RENAUDAIS, warehouse guard at Terre Blanc
PASCAL, captain of the company's brigatine
CARON, captain of the company's boat
La LOIRE des URSINS, former councillor
SABANIER, his wife, one child
VILLENEUVE, his wife, one child
LOUIS MIRAULT dit St. LOUIS, tailor, his child
LOUIS La TORTILLIER dit La MARCHE, his wife
          and his child
ANTOINE GAVIGNON dit FRAPE du BORD, his
          two children
LIVERNAIS , his wife, one child
JULIEN CHARTIER
JEAN DESPACE dit BEAUSEJOUR, his child
JEAN CHARLES Le MAIRE dit CAMBRELOT
LOUIS HENRY dit PETIT LOUIS, 2 children
PICARD, his wife and son in law, coppersmith
LEONARD
CHARANTE and four children
ANTOINE JOUARD dit MOUTON
JEAN GEORGE SCHUTZ dit JEAN l'ALLEMAND
JEAN ROUSSIN, child
PIERRE BILLY dit La JEUNESSE
JOSEPH DUCROT, cooper for the company
PIERRE DAUVIDO dit Le BLEU
La FORC, wife
GRIMAULT La PLAIN, wife and neice

A-29

Le HOUX, child and neice, former warehouse
            guard at Arkansas
ANSELME FOUCAULT dit La FLEUR
FRANCOIS CENSIER
JEAN DELON
FRANCOIS FERTIN, 2 children, brother in law
GABRIEL POULIN
l'EVESQUE, child
PIERRE LAMBREMONT, child
JEAN LOUIS DUPIN
JEAN FLANDRIN, wife, 2 children
the wife of MICHEL BEAU
PAPIN, interpreter, wife, 2 children
LOUIS LONGUEVILLE
La FERTE
JEAN EVRARD, a bohemian
STROUP, a bohemian, wife, child
ESTIENNE RENE
LARTOUT, tailor
BIDEAU, wife, child
PONCORET, wife, 2 children
MODESTE
Le BRASSEUR, the brewer, wife
BARBIER
MASSIOT
the wife of CANTRELLE, midwife
GUERIN, wife, 2 children
the wife of SONDU, goldsmith, and child
PIMIN ROBINET
DUCHESNE, of the Invalides
QUIDOR and PIERRE, his servants
FOULIAN, wife, child
Le CLERC, wife
the nehphew of de LONGRAIS
Madame, commander of the negroes at Terre Blanc
POUVALIN, wife, child
ROBICHON, wife, child
AUBERLET, wife, child
PIERRE SCHMITT, wife, child, brother in law
GASPARD TILLY, wife, 2 children, brother
ROSSER, wife, child
La DOUCEUR
the child of NICOLAS La COUR
Le GRAND, mason, wife, 2 children
SANS SOUCY, servant of GUYOT
ESTIENE, blacksmith for M., de LONGRAIS
                     A-29

the wife of MIRLY and child
PIERRE Le BLANC
DUCORROIR, cooper
PASCAL, cooper
La LANDE
GOUPIL
BONAVENTURE
La VIEILLE ( a bohemian knight)
La MIETTE, 3 children
JOLY, cabinet maker, wife
Le COEUR, cabinet maker, wife
LEGER, cabinet maker, wife
ISBRA, carpenter
BAPTISTE, carpenter
JEAN JOUAN, carpenter
RIBERT, carpenter
PICARD, carpenter
MONTHUY, wife, child
PIERRE TOUDOU, wife, child
BEAUSOLEIL, servant of SABANIER
CORNSERET, cooper
widow of RICHARD, child
PIERRE LETANT
BENICHON
BADEAU
Le MAIRE, cooper
DAUPHINE ( a woman)
MONTAUBAN, ( a woman), 2 children
ALAIN DUQUAY ditLe Petit MASON
FRANCOIS HYACINTHE
GILLES JOSSIAN
La PIERRE dit CHATALAIN

The following were travellers from New Orleans and
were also killed
Reverend JOSEPH POISSON, jesuit missionary
KOLY, and his son
LANGLOIS, clerk for Koly
CHARLOT VERLUG, son of Chapitoula
BOURBOIS, colonist of New Orleans
St. PIERRE, workman for BOURBEAU of New Orleans
SOUPAR of Yazoo
BOMPUGNON, of Yazoo
DuCODERE, commander at Yazoo

A-29

A detachment from Tunica, which included
MESPLET, who was tortured with DOMINIQUE
St. AMANT
BUSEBOIS
NAVARRE
LENNARD, a volunteer

* * * * * * * * * *

LIST OF PROPERTY OWNERS OF NEW ORLEANS
ON THE MAP PUBLISHED BY GONICHON IN 1731

Concession of M. KOLLY
BIENVILLE
Le sieur de BREUILLE
Concession of le Marquis d'ASFELD
Le sieur BONNEAU
Concession of M. PARIS at Bayougoulas
La CHAISE
TIXERAND
Succession of M. PAUGER
La FRESNIERE
Le sieur BELLISLE
Le sieur DELERI
Widow of MANDEVILLE
Le sieurs DREUX
Le sieur DAUSSEVILLE
Widow of DUVAL, and Le sieur BEAULIEU
Widow of DUVAL
Le sieur ROSSARD
Le sieur St. MARTIN
Le sieur DARBI
Le sieur de MONIE
Le sieur DELERI
Le sieur d'ARTACUET
PETIT de LIVILIER
Le sieur DAMARON
Le sieur PELLARIN
Le sieur GAUVRIT
Madame PROVANCHET
De VILLEUR
Le sieur LAZOU
Le sieur RAGUET
Le sieur TRUDOT
Le sieur Le BLANC
Le sieur MORAND
DAUBLIN
AUFRAIRE
Le sieur MORISSET
VANDOME
Le sieur BRULE
BRUSLE
MANADET
St. HILLAIRE
VALLERANT

A-31

SARAZIN
VITRI
PIGRI
widow of La GOUBLAYE
COUPARD
Widow of JARI
FAVRE
La FRENIERE
Succession of La TOUR
de LATTE
ARNAU DROYE dit BELLAIRE
CHAMILLY
BEAUSEJOUR
OZANE
SANFASSON
RIVARD
LOUBOIS
Widow of TREPANIER
JOSEPH CARRIERE
HAURY
FRANÇOIS CARRIERE
CARON
MARIN
ALLIN
Le NORMAND
AUGUSTIN l'ANGLOIS
widow of RIVARD
The capuchin fathers
Le sieur ARNAUD
MOREAU
MALO
DRIAND
BARASSON
MALO
BLANCVILLIA
widow of ROBERT
CHAVANNE
widow of CARDINAL
BIGOT
d'ALCOUR
widow of CARPENTRAS
du SABLON
BRETONNE
GRANDJEAN
Le GRAND COUR

A-31

MONROUGE
La PIERRE
St. MARTIN
LIVAUDAIS
MORISSET
CHEMITTE
demoiselle BONPART
Le sieur ALEXANDRE
CHEMITTE
BONNET
DAUVILLE
CHASTANT
children of AUDROVIN
La LIBERTE
TRONQUIDI
widow of La VIGNE
St. HILLAIRE
La ROSE ( the brewer)
MICHAL
l'EMPILLEUR
SAUTIER
ROCHER
ROBERT
DURANTAI
FONDER
Le MAIRE
ROBERT
PAULE VITRAE
MARIE FRANCOISE ( a woman)
COMMERCY
THOMAS
SENET
AVIGNON
FRANCOEUR
widow of F. SAUSSIER
VANDOME
FORESTIER
DARGARET
ROUSSEAU and FONDER
La RIVIERE
PINET
Le MARIE
Du PART
JEAN LOUIS
La COSTE and the woman MARIE FRANCOISE
ORLEANS

A-31

CHENIER
MANCELLIERE
CHENIER
JOSEPH
BRIGNARD
BALNE
l'AUVERGNAT
MARIE ( a negress)
BRUNET
BOURBON
La MAURI
La BOUCHARDIERE
POIRE
BROUET
St. JOSEPH
GUIDOU
VINCENT and CAPE
FLARON
widow of CHARON
JELIZO ( a woman)
Le sieur VOISIN
MARIE TOURNEL ( a woman)
FILARD
CHAPRON
LAPALINE
St. JEAN
DESLORIERS
JEAN FOUTRE
THOMAS LEGER
REITER
La ROCHE CASTEL
BEQUET
BARBEAU
MANSEAU
FAVIER
St. JACQUES
MARTIN ( the miller)
CRISTINA
La CLEF
ROSSARD
CANEL
Le DUC
POUSSORT ( a woman)
PIERRE GAUTIER
La ROZE ALIX
GUILLAUTEL

A-31

SARROT
FILASSIER
PIERRE RENAUD
BROSSET
RAFFLOT
La PIERRE
MARTIN
widow of BAILLY
NEGRIER
TOURANGEAU
DUPRE
DAUSSEVILLE
MAROUSTIL
NICOLAS AUBRUN
BALLE
BRUNELLE
JADELA
BOTSUN
FLAMANT
l'ARTEAU
du BUISSON
MOIN
GRATIEN LANTIER
BOURGUIGNON
LAMBERT
LOYSEL
La ROZE
BOURGUIGNON ( a woman)
MARCHE PITERRE
NICOLAS FAUIER
FRANCOIS RENFUREAU
FRANCOIS CHEVEAU
l'ARCHE
HUPE
NANTIER
GUILLAUME FAUCHER
JULIEN GAUTIER
BOURGUIGNON
l'EMPILLEUR
St. GERMAN
l'EMPILLEUR
PARISIEN
St. MICHEL
BELLEROZE
LANTUREU
REINE ( a woman)
l'ARCHE

A-31

NOTES ON THE CENSUS TABLE OF 1731 FOR THE
BANKS OF THE MISSISSIPPI RIVER

This census includes those inhabitants who occupy the banks
of the Mississippi river, from its source to a point some-
what above the present state line separating Louisiana and
Mississippi.

The census, as originally presented, shows two columns for
inhabitants, the first being "habitants and concessions",
the second being the name of the principal inhabitant. In
most cases these names are the same in both columns, so that
this writer combined the two columns. An asterix next to a
name signifies that this name appears in the first column
as concession owner, the name following is the occupant, if
shown. No asterix signifies that the owner was the habitant.

Following are seven of the original 12 columns, giving the
"human element" of the population of these concessions,
the headings being as follows:
   W, women and marriagable girls. When a 1, this usually
signifies the wife of the occupant.
   C, children of both sexes
   E, european workers, not named, of both sexes
   M, men capable of bearing arms. This would be the
individual named in the first column as habitant, unless
more than 1, which would then include his elder sons.
   NS, signifies negro slaves of both sexes
   NC, signifies negro children of both sexes
   IS signifies indian slaves of both sexes.

The census tabulates as follows:
| | |
|---|---|
| women and marriagable girls | 209 |
| children of the family | 390 |
| european engagees | 119 |
| men capable of bearing arms | 377 |
| negro slaves | 2529 |
| negro children | 819 |
| indian slaves | 47 |

The remainder of the table, not included above, tabulated
horses (265), sheep (2934), horned cattle (254), goats (10),
and guns (503).

CENSUS OF INHABITANTS ALONG THE RIVER
MISSISSIPPI DATED 1731, (unsigned but initialled
by N.S.)

| Inhabitant | W | C | E | M | NS | NC | IS |
|---|---|---|---|---|---|---|---|
| MADRE | 1 | 1 | | 1 | 2 | | |
| CONTANT | 1 | 1 | | 1 | | | |
| FLOU | 1 | 4 | | 1 | 1 | | 1 |
| La RIBARDIE | | | | 1 | | | |
| Le sieur TRONQUILLY | 1 | 3 | | 1 | 4 | 1 | |
| ROBIN | 1 | 1 | 2 | 3 | 11 | 6 | |
| FAUCHEUX | 1 | 2 | | | | | |
| JOLICOEUR | 1 | 2 | 2 | 3 | 1 | | |
| Le sieur MONTIGNY | 1 | 3 | | 1 | 2 | 1 | |
| CASTEL | 1 | | | 1 | | | |
| BEAUPRE | 1 | 1 | | 1 | 2 | | |
| DRAPEAU | 1 | 2 | 1 | 2 | 3 | | |
| BUISSON | 1 | 2 | | 1 | 8 | 1 | |
| JACQUES PERIER | 1 | | 1 | 2 | 16 | 1 | |
| PINET | 1 | | 1 | 1 | 5 | 1 | |
| PASQUIER | 1 | 2 | | 1 | 1 | | |
| l'EMPILEUR* | | | | | 7 | | |
| SAUCIER* | | | | | | | |
| Le sieur ARNAUD | | | | 1 | 10 | 1 | |
| Trudeau's sons* | | | | | | | |
| Le sieur TRUDEAU | | | | 1 | 7 | 4 | |
| widow SAUCIER | 1 | 3 | | | 7 | 3 | |
| MEUNIER | | | | 1 | 4 | 4 | |
| Le sieur JACQUES CARRIER | | 1 | | 1 | 8 | 7 | 1 |
| Le sieur FRANCOIS CARRIER | 1 | 3 | 3 | 4 | 17 | 17 | 4 |
| Le sieur JOSEPH CARRIER | 1 | 4 | | 1 | 12 | 10 | |
| Le sieur TISSERANT | 1 | 5 | 1 | 2 | 33 | 12 | 2 |
| BOYER | | | 1 | 2 | 33 | 12 | 2 |
| CHEVAL | | | | 1 | 12 | 7 | 1 |
| FRANCOIS PERALBE | | | | 1 | 1 | | |
| Le sieur FILART | | | | 1 | 8 | 1 | |
| Le sieur BRUSLE | | | | 1 | 5 | 2 | |
| LIVET | 1 | 4 | | 1 | 7 | 2 | |
| LEONARD | 1 | | | 1 | 6 | 1 | |
| CHAMILLY | | | | 1 | 4 | 2 | |
| BACHEMIN CORBIN | 1 | 7 | | 1 | 4 | 1 | |

B-31

| Inhabitant | W | C | E | M | NS | NC | IS |
|---|---|---|---|---|---|---|---|
| La LOIRE JOUSSET | 1 | 4 | | 1 | 7 | 3 | 1 |
| CHAPERON | 1 | | | 1 | 15 | 5 | |
| FLEURIE | | | | 1 | 4 | 4 | |
| RICARD | | | | 1 | 4 | | |
| LOUBOEY* | | | | | | | |
| La PRADE | 1 | | | 1 | 1 | | |
| VAUPARIS* | | | | | 5 | 1 | |
| La LIBERTE | 1 | | | 1 | 14 | | |
| The reverend Capuchin fathers* | | | | | 5 | | |
| Le sieur DESMORIERS | | | | 1 | 1 | | |
| Le sieur DARBONNE | 1 | 3 | | 1 | 2 | 1 | |
| DAUSSEVILLE* | | | 1 | 1 | 25 | 10 | |
| Religious order* Le sieur VAUPARIS | 1 | | | 1 | 16 | 3 | |
| St. MARTIN* | | | 1 | 1 | 17 | 9 | 1 |
| Le sieur FLEURIAR Attorney general | 1 | 2 | 1 | 2 | 16 | 8 | 1 |
| BROUTIN | 1 | 3 | 1 | 1 | 34 | 14 | 2 |
| Le sieur RAGUET | 1 | 2 | 1 | 2 | 15 | 3 | |
| Le sieur MAREST de la TOUR | | | | 1 | 7 | 1 | 2 |
| Le sieur MAREST DUPUY | 1 | | | 1 | 8 | 3 | |
| Le sieur DALCOURT* | 1 | 6 | | 1 | 30 | 14 | |
| and Demoiselle MILON | 1 | | | | | | |
| Succession of sieur La CHAISE* Le sieur BISOTON | | | | | 29 | 8 | |
| GAUVRIT* | 1 | 2 | | | 7 | 3 | 1 |
| Le sieur TRUDEAU senior | | | | 1 | 30 | 23 | |
| La BOULAY* | 1 | 2 | | | 11 | 6 | |
| Le sieur COUSTILLAS | | | | 1 | 38 | 17 | |
| Le sieur des KAIRAC | | | | 1 | 6 | 1 | |
| DARBY LAINE* DARBY | | | | 1 | 10 | 1 | |
| DREUX* | | | | 1 | 3 | 2 | |

note: The above were on the river below
New Orleans. The census compiler notes this
by a note to the effect that the city is
now encountered, which he does not list.
B-31

| Inhabitant | W | C | E | M | NS | NC | IS |
|---|---|---|---|---|---|---|---|
| Continuation is now along the right bank ascending listing inhabitants starting at the city of New Orleans upper limits. | | | | | | | |
| The reverend Jesuit fathers* | | | 2 | 2 | 29 | 13 | |
| The brick manufacture | | | | | 15 | | |
| of d'HAUTERIVES* | | | 1 | 1 | 36 | 2 | |
| Succession of VILLAINVILLE* | | | | | 7 | | 1 |
| DARBY cadet* | | | | | 2 | | |
| BONNAUD* | | | | | 12 | 6 | |
| DAUPHIN senior* | | | | | 8 | 1 | |
| DAUPHIN sons* | 1 | 1 | | 1 | 6 | | |
| LIVAUDAIS* | | | 1 | 1 | 12 | 4 | |
| LOUIS ROYE | 1 | 4 | 1 | 2 | 2 | | |
| VOISIN* occupant BORE | | | | 1 | 6 | 3 | |
| Le sieur de BLANC | 1 | | 1 | 2 | 8 | 5 | |
| Le sieur PASQUIET | | | | | 10 | 2 | |
| Le sieur BELLAIRE | 1 | 3 | | 1 | 22 | 13 | |
| BLANPIN* | | 4 | | 4 | 9 | 1 | 2 |
| Le sieur CHAVANNES | | | | 1 | 26 | 9 | 1 |
| ADAM dit BLOUDIN | 1 | | | 1 | 4 | | |
| PRADEL* | | | | | 6 | | |
| Continuation, at Chapitoulas | | | | | | | |
| GUYOT* with | 1 | 1 | | 1 | 5 | | |
| St. GERMAIN | | | | 1 | | | |
| Concession of Du BREUIL* with | | | | | | | |
| Le sieur DUBREUIL | | | | | | | |
| Du BREUIL elder son | | | | | | | |
| Du BREUIL cadet | 1 | | 4 | 7 | 76 | 30 | |
| Concession of De LERY*with | | | | | | | |
| Le sieur de LERY | | | | | | | |
| De LERY elder son | | | | | | | |
| De LERY 2nd son | | | | | | | |
| De LERY 3rd son | 1 | 3 | 1 | 5 | 58 | 10 | |
| Le sieur de MOUY | 1 | 5 | | 1 | 59 | 15 | 2 |
| Le sieur La FRENIERE | 1 | 4 | 6 | 7 | 76 | 36 | 4 |
| Le sieur Le SUEUR | | | | 1 | | | |
| Concession of KOLLY * | | | 1 | 1 | 46 | 35 | |

| Inhabitant | W | C | E | M | NS | NC | IS |
|---|---|---|---|---|---|---|---|
| Continuation at Cannes Brulees ( Burnt Canes) | | | | | | | |
| JOSEPH VERET | 1 | 2 | 1 | 2 | 8 | 2 | |
| CANTEREL | 1 | 3 | 1 | 2 | 4 | 1 | |
| DARTAGUIETTE* | | | 2 | 2 | 39 | 24 | |
| Le sieur ISET | | | | 1 | 4 | 1 | |
| Concession of | | | | | | | |
| DARTAIGNAN* | | | | | | | |
| occupant Le sieur | | | | | | | |
| GALIMACHE | 1 | | 1 | 2 | 58 | 13 | |
| ANDRE CRETZ | 1 | 2 | | 1 | 3 | 1 | |
| JAMBART LIONNAIS | 1 | 2 | | 1 | 1 | | |
| DULUDE | | 1 | | 1 | 7 | 2 | 1 |
| NOYON | | | | 1 | 4 | | |
| SANSON | 1 | | 1 | 2 | 6 | 2 | |
| St. AMANT* | 1 | 2 | | | 4 | 1 | |
| ANTOINE ROUX | 1 | 3 | | 1 | 1 | | |
| FAVROT* | | | | | 2 | | |
| MAU | | | | 1 | 5 | 2 | |
| Occupants at a place called " Old Bustard" | | | | | | | |
| ROUSSEAU | 1 | 3 | | 1 | 8 | 1 | |
| La COSTE | 1 | | | 1 | 3 | | |
| German occupants at " Old Bustard" | | | | | | | |
| TOUPS and 2 | | | | | | | |
| grandsons | 1 | | | 3 | 3 | | |
| AMBROISE HEILD | 1 | 2 | 1 | 2 | 3 | | |
| PIERRE BROU | 1 | 3 | | 1 | 3 | | |
| JEAN BOURGEOIS | 1 | 3 | 1 | 2 | 1 | | |
| DAUPHINE | 1 | | | 1 | 1 | | |
| FRANCOIS CHEVAL | 1 | 5 | | 1 | 4 | 2 | |
| BORNES | 2 | 3 | 4 | 5 | 4 | | |
| RENE DORVIEINKS | | | | | | | |
| and his brother | 1 | | | 2 | 1 | | |
| POMMIER | 1 | 1 | | 1 | 2 | | |
| NICOLAS WITNER | 1 | 1 | | 1 | 2 | | |
| JOSEPH QUINTREL | | | | | | | |
| dit DUPONT | 1 | 5 | | 1 | 1 | | |
| DANIEL LOF | 1 | 2 | | 1 | 3 | | |
| PHILIPPE DOUAY | 1 | 3 | | 1 | 2 | | |
| JACQUES POCHE | | | | | | | |
| dit La CHAPELLE | 1 | 1 | | 1 | | | |
| MONTPIERRE | 1 | 5 | | 1 | 2 | | |

| Inhabitant | W | C | E | M | NS | NC | IS |
|---|---|---|---|---|---|---|---|

Continuation at Oumas ( The village of the Houma indians, the present site of Angola on the present state line between Louisiana and Mississippi.)

| Inhabitant | W | C | E | M | NS | NC | IS |
|---|---|---|---|---|---|---|---|
| FRANCOIS LEGRAS | 1 | 1 | | 1 | 2 | | 1 |
| PERRET | 1 | 1 | | 1 | 1 | | 1 |
| ROMAN | | | 5 | 6 | 5 | 1 | |
| CHAMPIGUOLS | 1 | 2 | | 1 | 2 | | |
| BARON | 1 | 2 | | 1 | 7 | 3 | |
| MAIGRE | 1 | | | 1 | | | |

Continuation at Ecores Blancs (white earth)

| Inhabitant | W | C | E | M | NS | NC | IS |
|---|---|---|---|---|---|---|---|
| MAIGRE | | | | 1 | 15 | 7 | 1 |

Continuation at Pointe Coupee ( Cut point, a bend in the River situated near the present Louisiana - Mississippi state line).

| Inhabitant | W | C | E | M | NS | NC | IS |
|---|---|---|---|---|---|---|---|
| COUILLARD | 1 | | | 1 | 2 | 3 | |
| JAPPIOT | 1 | | | 1 | 2 | 2 | |
| MICHEL BAU | 1 | | | 1 | 4 | 1 | |
| JEAN BARA | 1 | 1 | | 1 | 1 | | |
| La COUR | 1 | 2 | | 1 | 2 | 1 | |
| La FACINNE | | | | 1 | 1 | | |
| Le GROS | 1 | 1 | | 1 | | | |

At this point the compiler crosses the Mississippi River and commences to take the census of those on the other ( left) bank, in descending order, that is starting at Pointe Coupee and proceeding toward New Orleans.

| Inhabitant | W | C | E | M | NS | NC | IS |
|---|---|---|---|---|---|---|---|
| DUPONT | 1 | 1 | 1 | 2 | 2 | | |
| MATELOT | | | | 1 | 1 | | |
| AVIGNON | 1 | | | 1 | 1 | | |
| GAUSSERAU | 1 | 2 | | 1 | 1 | | |
| BONHOMME | | | | 1 | | | |
| Le COUREUR | 1 | | | 1 | | | |
| RAIMOND | 1 | | | 1 | 3 | | |
| BERGERON | 1 | | | 1 | 3 | | |
| CASTILLON | 1 | | | 1 | 1 | | |
| GUICHARD | 1 | | | 1 | 1 | | |
| GERMAIN | 1 | | | 1 | 9 | | 1 |
| DUPLECHIN | 1 | 1 | | | | | |
| Le NORMAND | 1 | 3 | | 1 | 2 | | |
| MAYEUX | 1 | 3 | | 1 | 1 | | |
| SOISSONS | 1 | 1 | | 1 | 4 | | |
| HOUMAR | 1 | 3 | | 1 | 2 | | |
| RONDEAU | 1 | 2 | | 1 | 4 | | 1 |

B-31

| Inhabitants | W | C | E | M | NS | NC | IS |
|---|---|---|---|---|---|---|---|
| Continuation, left bank, second department | | | | | | | |
| JEAN de CUIR | | | | 1 | 1 | 1 | |
| De CUIR senior | | | 1 | 2 | 4 | 2 | |
| ANOTIAU | 1 | 2 | | 1 | 3 | | 1 |
| HAUSSY | 1 | | | 1 | 2 | 1 | |
| widow ALLARD | 1 | 3 | 1 | 1 | | 1 | |
| widow Le PERCHE | 1 | | | | | | |
| BIENVENAU | | | | 1 | | | |
| HAYNAU | | | | | | | |
| ALAIN | | | | 1 | 1 | | |
| De COUX | 1 | 1 | 2 | 3 | 2 | | |
| Continuation, at Chetimachas ( indian village) | | | | | | | |
| Du SABLAY* | | | | 1 | 4 | | 1 |
| BELLEHUMEUR* | 1 | 1 | | 1 | 2 | | |
| CORDONIER* | 1 | | | 1 | 1 | | |
| JOUBART* | | | | 1 | 1 | | |
| LANDERNAU* | 1 | 2 | | 1 | | | |
| MARON* | 1 | 2 | | 1 | 1 | | |
| Continuation, at Bayagoulas ( indian village) | | | | | | | |
| Le sieur Du BUISSON MONFERIER | 1 | 5 | 1 | | 2 | 6 | |
| Le sieur La GARDE | | | 5 | 6 | 48 | 34 | 1 |
| Continuation, the German Villages | | | | | | | |
| JEAN MARTIN LAMBERT | 1 | 1 | | 1 | | | |
| MIKEL FOUQUEL | 1 | 2 | | 1 | 1 | | |
| FRANCOIS GAULOIS | 1 | 1 | | 1 | 1 | | |
| MIKEL HORN | 1 | | | 1 | | | |
| ETIENNE QUISTEMAKER | 1 | 1 | 1 | 2 | 1 | | |
| KALENDRE | 1 | 1 | | 1 | 1 | | |
| JEAN ROUSSEL | 1 | 3 | | 1 | | | |
| FREDERIC COURARD | 1 | 1 | 1 | 2 | 2 | | |
| BERNARD HUIKS | 1 | 2 | 1 | 2 | 1 | | |
| ALBERT | 1 | 1 | | 1 | 1 | | |
| GUILLAUME SIRIAK | 1 | | | 1 | | | |
| JEAN GEORGES POK | 1 | 3 | | 1 | | | |
| ANDRE CHANTS | 1 | 2 | | 1 | 3 | 1 | |
| BALTAZAR MARCK | 1 | 2 | | 1 | 1 | | |
| LEONARD MACKDOLF | 1 | | | 1 | | | |
| ADAM MATERNE | 1 | 3 | | 1 | 3 | | |
| JACQUES REITHER | 1 | | | 1 | | | |
| NICOLAS MAYER | 2 | 1 | 1 | 2 | 1 | 1 | |
| Le sieur DARENSBOURG | 1 | 4 | 1 | 2 | 3 | 3 | |
| ANDRE DREIKER | 1 | 3 | | 1 | 2 | | |
| The presbitary of the Capuchin priests | | | 3 | 4 | 1 | | |

B-31

120

| Inhabitants | W | C | E | M | NS | NC | IS |
|---|---|---|---|---|---|---|---|
| SIMON BERLIN | 1 | | | 1 | | | |
| Le sieur VENDERHEK | 1 | 1 | | 1 | 5 | 1 | |
| PIERRE MUNIK | 1 | 2 | | 1 | | | |
| ANDRE STRUNFS | 1 | 3 | | 1 | | | |
| Le sieur De LAIRE | | | | 1 | 2 | | |
| JOSEPH VAGUERSBAC | 1 | 3 | | 1 | 1 | 1 | |
| MATHIS FREDERIC | 1 | 3 | | 1 | | | |
| JACQUES FOLET | 1 | 2 | | 1 | | | |
| BERNARD ANTOINE | 1 | 3 | 1 | 2 | | | |
| CRISTIANNE CREBERT | 1 | 3 | | 1 | | | |
| ANDRE OFMAN | 1 | 4 | | 1 | | | |
| JACQUES OUBERT | 1 | 2 | 1 | 2 | 2 | | |
| GEORGES REUZER | 1 | 1 | | 1 | | | |
| GEORGES TROUCHELER | 1 | 2 | | 1 | 1 | 1 | |
| JEAN ADAM | 1 | 5 | | 1 | 1 | | |
| LIONNOIS | 1 | 1 | | 1 | | | |
| JACQUES RABLAU | 1 | 5 | | 1 | | | |

Continuation at " Old Bustard"

| | W | C | E | M | NS | NC | IS |
|---|---|---|---|---|---|---|---|
| SAINTON | 1 | 4 | | 1 | 5 | 2 | |
| LABE | 1 | 4 | | 1 | 9 | 3 | |
| DAVID * with | 1 | | | | | | |
| PARISIEN | 1 | | 1 | 3 | 5 | | |
| GASPARD | 1 | 2 | | 1 | 3 | | |
| La VERGUE | 1 | 3 | | 1 | 2 | | |
| JEAN DESLANDES | 1 | | | 1 | 5 | 1 | |
| PHILIPPE SOM | 1 | 3 | | 1 | 1 | | |
| CLERANT | 1 | | | 1 | 2 | | |
| La THULIPPE | | | | 1 | | | |
| FRANÇOIS DAUNAY | 1 | 2 | | 1 | | | |
| CRISTIANNE | 1 | 5 | | 1 | | | |
| JACQUES ROZIER | | | | 1 | | | |
| JACQUES KRESMANE | 1 | 1 | | 1 | | | |
| ANDRE KRESMANNE | 1 | 1 | 1 | 2 | 4 | | |
| DUPRE | 1 | 2 | | 3 | | | |

Concessions opposite Jannes Brulees

| | W | C | E | M | NS | NC | IS |
|---|---|---|---|---|---|---|---|
| LANGEVIN | 1 | | | 1 | 1 | | |
| PUGEOL | 1 | 3 | | 1 | 3 | | |
| SIMON COUE | 1 | 1 | | 1 | | | |
| DUPUY GOUPILLON | 1 | 3 | | 1 | 5 | | |
| Le sieur CHER de St. JULLIEN | | | 1 | 2 | 17 | | |
| La VERGUE | 1 | 5 | | 1 | 4 | | |
| QUERNION* | | | | 1 | 4 | | |
| BAILLIF* | 1 | | | 1 | 1 | | |
| Le sieur PETIT | 1 | 4 | 1 | 2 | 31 | | |

B-31

| Inhabitants | W | C | E | M | NS | NC | IS |
|---|---|---|---|---|---|---|---|
| Continuation, concessions opposite Chapitoulas | | | | | | | |
| The mill of | | | | | | | |
| Sieur De LERY* | 1 | | | | 3 | | |
| MIKEL SERINGUE | 1 | 3 | 1 | 2 | 12 | 4 | |
| Concession of | | | | | | | |
| DASFELD* | 1 | 1 | 2 | 2 | 12 | 3 | |
| FRANCOIS SENET | | | 1 | 2 | 13 | 2 | |
| SCIPION, free negro | | | | 1 | | | |
| SIMON, free negro | 1 | | | 1 | 1 | | |
| Le sieur PETIT | 1 | 1 | 1 | 2 | 16 | 1 | |
| Le sieur St. THERESE | | | | | | | |
| de LANGLOISERIE | | | | 1 | 11 | 8 | 2 |
| RISTENER sons | | | | 1 | 3 | | |
| JUDICE | 2 | 3 | 1 | 2 | 6 | 1 | |
| LARCHE, grandfather | 1 | | | 1 | 6 | 1 | |
| ETIENNE DAIGLE | 1 | 3 | | 1 | 5 | 2 | |
| VIGER | 1 | 4 | | 1 | 11 | 3 | |
| BIRNON | 1 | 4 | | 1 | 7 | 1 | |
| JOSEPH LARCHE | 2 | 1 | 1 | 2 | 10 | 1 | |
| LARCHE LAINE | 1 | 5 | | 1 | 15 | 4 | |
| The mill belonging to | | | | | | | |
| the succession of | | | | | | | |
| La CHAISE | 1 | 2 | 1 | 1 | 12 | | |
| PERIER *, occupant | | | | | | | |
| Le sieur LANGE | | | 1 | 2 | 72 | 25 | |
| Property of the Company of the Indes,* | | | | | | | |
| occupant Le sieur | | | | | | | |
| Le PAGE | | | 2 | 3 | 201 | 29 | |
| BOURGEOIS | 2 | 2 | 1 | 2 | 9 | | |
| Property of M. de | | | | | | | |
| BIENVILLE *, | | | | | | | |
| occupant SERVAY | | | | 1 | 33 | 36 | |
| BALDY | | | 1 | 2 | 10 | 2 | |
| PROVENCHE | 1 | | 2 | 3 | 7 | 7 | |
| AUGUSTIN LANGLOIS | 1 | 4 | 2 | 3 | 6 | 2 | |
| ETIENNE LANGLOIS | 1 | 5 | | 1 | 15 | 5 | 1 |
| LOUIS LANGLOIS | | | | 1 | 5 | 1 | |
| DUGUAY* | | | 1 | 1 | 24 | 4 | |
| MICHEL VIEN | 1 | 1 | 1 | 2 | 4 | | |
| JACQUES CHAUVIN | | | | 1 | 1 | | |
| PLAISANCE | 1 | 2 | 1 | 2 | 5 | 3 | |
| BEAUME | 2 | 4 | | 1 | 10 | 5 | |
| Le sieur FAZENDE | 2 | 3 | 1 | 2 | 15 | 8 | |
| PELLERIN* occupant | | | | | | | |
| Le sieur JAUGE | 2 | 3 | 1 | 2 | 20 | 8 | |

| Inhabitants | W | C | E | M | NS | NC | IS |
|---|---|---|---|---|---|---|---|
| PAUL BARRE | 1 | 2 | | 1 | 5 | 2 | |
| COUSSINNE | 1 | 4 | | 1 | 2 | | |
| FLEURIE *,occupant | | | | | | | |
|   PIERRE BONNE | | | | 1 | 3 | | |
| GRACE*, occupant | | | | | | | |
|   RODOLPHE | | | | 1 | 5 | | |
| Le sieur MARSILLY | 3 | 4 | | 1 | 23 | 9 | |
| FRANCOIS TREPANIER | | | | 1 | | | |
| Le sieur LABRO | 1 | 3 | | 1 | 17 | 13 | 1 |
| IGNACE TREPANIER | | | | 1 | 4 | 1 | |
| Concession of St. | | | | | | | |
|   Reine,*occupant | | | | | | | |
|   Le sieur DUMANOIR | | 2 | 1 | 2 | 27 | 8 | 3 |
| Concession of | | | | | | | |
|   DASFELD*, occupant | | | | | | | |
|   ROUJOT | 1 | 4 | 4 | 5 | 98 | 24 | |
| ROCQUINY | 1 | 3 | 1 | 2 | 8 | 1 | |
| Le sieur MASSY | 1 | | 2 | 3 | 30 | 21 | |
| THOMELAIN | | | | | 1 | | |
| DREUX cadet | | | | 1 | 10 | 7 | |
| HARANG | | | | 1 | 1 | | |
| PRAT*, occupant | | | | | | | |
|   MAINGURE | | | | 1 | 27 | 6 | |
| Capuchin fathers* | | | | | | | |
|   occupant | | | | | | | |
|   GUILLAUME | 1 | 2 | | 1 | 10 | 1 | |
| RIVARD, widow | 1 | 4 | 1 | 1 | 16 | 9 | |
| RIVARD sons | 1 | | | | | | |
| JOSEPH GIRARDY | 1 | 3 | | 1 | 15 | 7 | |
| TOURENJEAU* | | 2 | | 1 | 3 | 2 | |
| BOISSIER | 1 | | | 1 | 10 | | |
| Le sieur MORAND | 1 | | | 1 | 45 | 3 | |

\* \* \* \* \* \* \* \* \* \*

## NOTES ON THE CENSUS OF NEW ORLEANS FOR
## JANUARY 1732

This census is actually a continuation of the preceeding
Census for the Inhabitants along the Mississippi River,
for 1731.

As originally presented, the census shows two columns, the
first being proprietors or property owners, the second
the inhabitants in the house, proprietor or renting, or
simply in residence there. The following shows the proprietor in parentheses, following are the names of those in
residence.

In the original there are 17 columns, showing as duplicated
in the following, men (M), women (W), children belonging
to the household (C), orphans  (O),-negro slaves, which
in the original are divided into male and female but
combined here (NS), negro children (NC), Indian slaves
which in the original are divided into male and female,
combined here (IS), and mulattoes (MU). The original
census also gave the number of horses, cows, bulls, other
cattle, large guns ( fusils) and hand guns (pistoles).

A recapitulation shows the following:

|                                   |     |     |
| --------------------------------- | --- | --- |
| men capable of bearing arms       | 229 |     |
| women and marriagable girls       | 169 |     |
| children                          | 183 |     |
| orphans                           | 45  |     |
| total of european origin          |     | 626 |
|                                   |     |     |
| negroes                           | 102 |     |
| negresses                         | 74  |     |
| negro children                    | 76  |     |
| indian men                        | 5   |     |
| indian women                      | 6   |     |
| mulattoes, men and women          | 6   |     |
| total non-european, mostly slaves |     | 267 |

The remainder of the tabulation included 14 horses,
13 bulls, 39 cows, 26 other cattle, 513 large guns,
25 hand guns.

A-32

CENSUS OF THE INHABITANTS AND PROPERTY
OWNERS OF NEW ORLEANS AS OF JANUARY 1732 ( unsigned but
initialled by N..S.)

| (Proprietor) and Inhabitants | M | W | C | O | NS | NC | IS | MU |
|---|---|---|---|---|---|---|---|---|
| 1. On the quay (wharf) | | | | | | | | |
| (The Hospital) | | | | | | | | |
| DUCHEMIN, nurse | 1 | | | | | | | |
| (The King) | | | | | | | | |
| M. PRAT, Doctor | 1 | 1 | | | 2 | 1 | | 1 |
| M. BIZOTON | 1 | | 1 | | | | | |
| (M. RAQUET) | | | | | | | | |
| (M. LAZOU) | | | | | | | | |
| M. LAZOU, captain | 1 | 1 | | 1 | 7 | | | |
| ( M. PELLERIN, warehouse guard) | | | | | | | | |
| M. PELLERIN | 1 | 1 | 2 | | 3 | 3 | | 1 |
| Made. PELLERIN | | 1 | | | | | | |
| Le sieur LANTHEAUME | 1 | | | | | | | |
| M. DESCHAMPS | 1 | | | | | | | |
| M. GAUTHEREAU | 1 | | | | 1 | | | |
| ( M. DAMARON, druggist) | | | | | | | | |
| M. DAMARON | 1 | | 2 | | 4 | | 1 | |
| Made. DAMARON | | 1 | | | | | | |
| (M. DARTAGUIETTE) | | | | | | | | |
| M. DARTAGUIETTE | | | | | | | 1 | 2 |
| M. de SALMON | 1 | | | | 2 | 3 | | |
| Made. SALMON | | 1 | | | | | | |
| Made. Le BRETON | | 1 | | | | | | |
| M. Le BRETON | 1 | | | | | | | |
| DERLIN, servant | 1 | | | | | | | |
| CHARLES, cook | 1 | | | | | | | |
| M. de La POMERAY, treasurer | 1 | | | | 1 | | | |
| M. PREFONTAINE | 1 | | | | | 1 | | |
| (Made. DHAUTERIVES) | | | | | | | | |
| Made. DHAUTERIVES | | 1 | 1 | | 2 | 1 | | |

A-32

| (Proprietor) and Inhabitants | M | W | C | O | NS | NC | IS | MU |
|---|---|---|---|---|---|---|---|---|
| (Succession of desc. M. DUVAL, of the service of the Company of the Indies) | | | | | | | | |
| M. PREVOST | 1 | | | | 6 | 2 | | |
| M. ARBAUD | 1 | | | | 1 | 1 | | |
| M. COUTURIER | 1 | | | | | | | |
| M. ADAM | 1 | | | | | | | |
| ( M. DAUSSEVILLE) | | | | | | | | |
| M. DAUSSEVILLE | 1 | | | | | | | |
| ( MICHEL) | | | | | | | | |
| MICHEL, baker | 1 | 1 | | 1 | 1 | | | |
| JEAN TOUZAY | 1 | | | | | | | |
| ( M. DREUX) | | | | | | | | |
| M. DREUX | 1 | | | | | | | |
| ( The King) | | | | | | | | |
| M. BROUTIN, engineer | 1 | | | | | | | |
| Le sieur SAUCIER, draftsman | 1 | | | | | | | |
| ( M. TIXERANT) | | | | | | | | |
| ( M. de la GARDE) | | | | | | | | |
| M. de TROHOIS, clerk of the company | 1 | | | | | | | |
| (For the DASFELD concession) | | | | | | | | |
| CAUSSY, financier | 1 | | | | 2 | | | |
| ( M. BONNAUD) | | | | | | | | |
| M. and Made. BONNAUD | 1 | 1 | 1 | | 2 | 2 | | |
| ( M. de NOYAN) | | | | | | | | |
| M. de NOYAN, Captain | 1 | | | | 3 | 1 | | |
| St. MARTIN, servant | 1 | | | | | | | |
| ( Mill of the King) | | | | | | | | |
| KPSERR, miller | 1 | 1 | 2 | | | | | |

A-32

| (Proprietor) and Inhabitants. | M | W | C | O | NS | NC | IS | MU |
|---|---|---|---|---|---|---|---|---|
| ( The Reverend Jesuit Fathers) | | | | | | | | |
| Rev. Father PETIT | 1 | | | | | | | |
| Father PARISET | 1 | | | | | | | |

2. Rue de Chartres
   ( Chartres Street)

| | M | W | C | O | NS | NC | IS | MU |
|---|---|---|---|---|---|---|---|---|
| ( Succession of KOLLY) six Ursuline sisters . | | | | | | | | |
| Six boarders , 27 orphans | | 9 | 3 | 27 | | | | |
| ( M. DUBREUIL) | | | | | | | | |
| Made. DUBREUIL | | 1 | | | 1 | | | |
| ( M. BRUSLE) | | | | | | | | |
| M. LEVAUDAIS, port captain | 1 | | | | | 2 | | |
| ( The King) | | | | | | | | |
| M. MANADE, surgeon | 1 | | | | | | | |
| Made. MANADE | | 1 | | | 6 | 6 | 2 | |
| ( For St. HILAIRE) | | | | | | | | |
| St. HILAIRE, carpenter | 1 | 1 | 2 | | 3 | | | |
| (VALLERAN) | | | | | | | | |
| VALLERAN, turner | 1 | 1 | 3 | | | | | |
| ( M. BORDELON) | | | | | | | | |
| Made. BORDELON | | 1 | 4 | | 1 | 1 | | |
| (VITRY) | | | | | | | | |
| FRANCOIS SONGY | 1 | 1 | 3 | | | | | |
| (PIQUERY) | | | | | | | | |
| PIQUERY, baker | 1 | 1 | 3 | 1 | 2 | 2 | | |
| (BELLAIRE) | | | | | | | | |
| BELLAIRE | 1 | 1 | 3 | | 1 | 2 | | |
| ( M. BALIOUS) | | | | | | | | |
| Made. PRADEL | | 1 | | | 1 | 2 | | |
| Le sieur LAYRAC | 1 | | | | | | | |

A-32

| (Proprietor) and Inhabitants | M | W | C | O | NS | NC | IS | MU |
|---|---|---|---|---|---|---|---|---|
| (THOMELAIN) THOMELAIN, joiner | 1 | 1 | 1 | | 4 | 1 | | |
| ( M. BRUSLE) Made. BRUSLE | | 1 | 1 | | 2 | 1 | | |
| M. BALCOUS, guard of the Fortifications | 1 | | | | 2 | | | |
| ( The Capuchin Priests) Rev. Father RAPHAEL, pastor Rev. Father HIACINTE Rev. father PIERRE | 3 | | | 2 | 2 | 2 | | |
| ( M. MARSILLY) M. PACQUET | 1 | | | | | | | |
| ( M. CARIER) M. MARQUIS, commissioner of the Company | 1 | | | | | | | |
| ( M. MARSILLY) M. HENRY, commissioner and attorney | 1 | 1 | | | | 1 | | |
| ( M. CARIERE ) FORCADE, tobacco inspector | 1 | | | | | | | |
| ( CARON) CARON, butcher | 1 | 1 | 1 | 1 | 2 | | | |
| ( M. ARNAUT) RUEL, mason | 1 | 1 | | | | | | |
| Widow HENRY | | 1 | | | | | | |
| ( MOREAU) Moreau | 1 | 1 | | | 1 | | 1 | |
| ( LOUIS BLARD dit St. LOUIS) LOUIS BLARD dit St. LOUIS | 1 | 1 | | | | | | |
| Widow DIRUAUCHE ( DIMANCHE?) | | 1 | | | | | | |
| ( CHARTIER) MULON, tailor | 1 | | | | | | | |

3
A-32

| (Proprietor) and Inhabitant | M | W | C | O | NS | NC | IS | MU |
|---|---|---|---|---|---|---|---|---|
| (Widow DRILLAN) Widow CHEVALIER | | 1 | | | | | | |
| ( the same) VEILLON, turner | 1 | | | | | | | |
| La BAPTISTE | | 1 | | | | | | |
| ( For PROVENCHE) BESSON | 1 | 1 | 2 | | | | | |
| La FONTAINE, tailor | 1 | | | | | | | |
| BOUTONNIER, former soldier | 1 | | | | | | | |
| TISON | 1 | | | | | 1 | | |
| (VILLEUR) VILLEUR | 1 | | | | | | | |
| ( The King) LEONARD, gardener and Intendant | 1 | 1 | | | | | | |
| FREDERIC LEONARD | 1 | | | | | | | |
| GEORGES CAP, cooper | 1 | | | | | | | |
| JACQUES ROYE | 1 | | | | | | | |
| ( Le MOINE) Le MOINE, joiner | 1 | 1 | 3 | | | | 1 | |
| PATIN, joiner | 1 | | | | | | | |
| ( BLANPIN) BLANPIN | 1 | | | | | | | |
| ( M. BROUTIN) M. AMELOT and SONGARION | 2 | | | | | | | |

3. Rue Royalle ( Royal Street)

| (Proprietor) and Inhabitant | M | W | C | O | NS | NC | IS | MU |
|---|---|---|---|---|---|---|---|---|
| (CHMIT) CHMIT | 1 | 1 | 3 | | | | | |
| ( The same) Made. de St. HERMINE | | 1 | 1 | | | | | |
| (BONNET) BONNET, Gardian of the park | 1 | 1 | | 1 | | | | |

A-32

| (Proprietor) and Inhabitant | M | W | C | O | NS | NC | IS | MU |
|---|---|---|---|---|---|---|---|---|
| (M. DAUVILLE) |  |  |  |  |  |  |  |  |
| M. Dauville | 1 | 1 | 2 |  | 2 | 1 |  |  |
| ( M. MICHEL) |  |  |  |  |  |  |  |  |
| M. MICHEL, commissioner of the King | 1 | 1 | 4 |  | 3 | 1 |  |  |
| (LEMPILEUR) |  |  |  |  |  |  |  |  |
| DUMAS dit LEMPILEUR | 1 | 1 | 2 |  |  |  |  |  |
| (BERTAUD) |  |  |  |  |  |  |  |  |
| BERTAUD, carpenter | 1 | 1 | 1 |  |  |  |  |  |
| (SAUTIER) |  |  |  |  |  |  |  |  |
| SAUTIER, joiner | 1 | 1 | 1 |  |  |  |  |  |
| MARIE, bohemian |  | 1 |  |  |  |  |  |  |
| ( for M. SAUCIE) |  |  |  |  |  |  |  |  |
| CARITON, tailor | 1 |  |  |  |  |  |  |  |
| POUSSINNE, tailor | 1 |  |  |  |  |  |  |  |
| MANSIAU, a boy | 1 |  |  |  |  |  |  |  |
| BOUTON | 1 |  |  |  |  |  |  |  |
| ( VENDOMIE) |  |  |  |  |  |  |  |  |
| VENDOME | 1 | 1 | 2 |  |  |  |  |  |
| (FORESTIER) |  |  |  |  |  |  |  |  |
| FORESTIER | 1 | 1 | 3 |  | 1 |  |  |  |
| (LEMAIRE) |  |  |  |  |  |  |  |  |
| LEMAIRE, Innkeeper | 1 |  |  |  | 2 |  |  |  |
| ELISABET, wife of La PIERRE |  | 1 |  |  |  |  |  |  |
| (JACQUET) |  |  |  |  |  |  |  |  |
| JACQUET | 1 | 1 | 2 |  |  |  |  |  |
| (children of MANIERE) |  |  |  |  |  |  |  |  |
| JOSEPH MARIE PATRON | 1 | 1 | 2 |  |  |  |  |  |
| (CHENIER) |  |  |  |  |  |  |  |  |
| CHENIER | 1 | 1 |  |  | 2 |  |  |  |
| (JOSEPH) |  |  |  |  |  |  |  |  |

A-32

| (Proprietor) and Inhabitant | M | W | C | O | NS | NC | IS | MU |
|---|---|---|---|---|---|---|---|---|
| (AVILLE) La BOUCHARDIERE | 1 | 1 | 1 | | | | | |
| (POIRE) POIRE, gunsmith | 1 | 1 | 2 | | | | | |
| (BROUET) BROUET, waggoner | 1 | 1 | 1 | | 2 | | | |
| PLAISANCE | 1 | 1 | 1 | | | | | |
| Widow of SANS CHAGRIN | | 1 | 1 | | | | | |
| (St. JOSEPH) St. JOSEPH | 1 | 1 | 3 | | 5 | | | |
| FRANCOIS | 1 | | | | | | | |
| ( M. VOISIN) M. VOISIN | 1 | | 5 | | 2 | 2 | | |
| his son | 1 | | | | | | | |
| ( widow of St. ANDRE) GIRAUD, joiner | 1 | 1 | 2 | | | | | |
| ( 3 houses bel. to M. VOISIN) | | | | | | | | |
| (M. CHAPRON) | | | | | | | | |
| (PANTINET) widow PANTINET, a bohemian | | 1 | 1 | | | | | |
| (DUSABLON) DUSABLON | 1 | 1 | | | | | | |
| ( BAPTISTE MOUTARD) BAPTISTE MOUTARD, joiner | 1 | 1 | 2 | | | | | |
| ( JEAN MERLE) JEAN MERLE | 1 | | | | | | | |
| ( La GRANDCOURT) VALADE, sailor | 1 | 1 | | | | | | |
| (FINEAU) FINEAU | 1 | 1 | 2 | 2 | 2 | | | |

A-32

| ( Proprietor) and Inhabitant | M | W | C | O | NS | NC | IS | MU |
|---|---|---|---|---|---|---|---|---|
| (BRUNET) BRUNET, blacksmith | 1 | | | | | | | |
| (AUBERT) | | | | | | | | |
| ( M. CHAVANNE) NICOLAS VISE ( VIU?) | 1 | 1 | 2 | | 2 | 1 | | |
| ( MONTAUBAN) ALAIN , former sailor | 1 | 1 | 1 | | | | | |
| (DROUILLON) DROUILLON | 1 | 1 | 3 | | 1 | | | |
| ( M. LANGLOIS) DARGURET, sheriff | 1 | 1 | 2 | | 1 | | | |
| ( BEAUSEJOUR) BARY, coppersmith | 1 | 1 | 1 | | | | | |
| JACQUES La RIVIERE, former sailor | 1 | | | | | | | |
| La TELLIER ( woman) | | 1 | | | | | | |
| (OZANNE) OZANNE, cooper | 1 | 1 | 2 | | 3 | | | |
| TESSON | 1 | | | | | | | |
| ( SANS FACON) | | | | | | | | |
| (JARRY) widow JARRY | | 1 | 3 | | 1 | 2 | | |
| (FABRE) FABRE, gunner | 1 | 1 | | | | | | |
| his mother in law | | 1 | | | | | | |
| (M. dela FRENIERE) Widow of LAVIOLETTE | | 1 | | | | | | |
| ( M. BRUSLE) | | | | | | | | |
| (BELLAIRE) BELLAIRE, carpenter | 1 | 1 | 5 | | | | | |

A-32

| ( Proprietor) and Inhabitant | M | W | C | O | NS | NC | IS | MU |
|---|---|---|---|---|---|---|---|---|
| ( M. MORICET) | | | | | | | | |
| DURIVAGE, macon | | | | | | | | |
| (DAUPHIN) | | | | | | | | |

4. Rue de Bourbon ( Bourbon street)

| ( Proprietor) and Inhabitant | M | W | C | O | NS | NC | IS | MU |
|---|---|---|---|---|---|---|---|---|
| (DAUPHIN) | | | | | | | | |
| Widow LAFORGE | | 1 | | | | | | |
| (widow La SONDE) | | | | | | | | |
| widow La SONDE | | 1 | 1 | | 1 | 1 | | |
| ( DESLAURIERS) | | | | | | | | |
| ( La ROCHE CASTEL) | | | | | | | | |
| La ROCHE CASTEL, blacksmith | 1 | 1 | 1 | | 1 | | | |
| (BECQUET) | | | | | | | | |
| BECQUET, locksmith | 1 | 1 | 3 | | 1 | | | |
| ( BARBAUD) | | | | | | | | |
| BARBAUD | 1 | 1 | 4 | | 5 | 1 | | |
| (MANICAU) | | | | | | | | |
| MANICAU | 1 | 1 | 2 | | | | | |
| ( La CLEF) | | | | | | | | |
| La CLEF, commander | 1 | 1 | 1 | | | | | |
| (CANELLE) | | | | | | | | |
| CANELLE, carpenter | 1 | 1 | | | | | | |
| (Le DUC) | | | | | | | | |
| Le DUC, locksmith | 1 | 1 | | | | | | |
| (BELHUMEUR) | | | | | | | | |
| BELHUMEUR | 1 | 1 | 3 | | 1 | | | |
| (GAUTIER) | | | | | | | | |
| GAUTIER, mason | 1 | 1 | | 1 | | | | |
| JEAN SADOT, former soldier | 1 | | | | | | | |

A-32

| ( Proprietor) and Inhabitant | M | W | C | O | NS | NC | IS | MU |
|---|---|---|---|---|---|---|---|---|
| ( La ROZE ALIX) | | | | | | | | |
| (RENAUDOT) RENAUDOT ..dit SANS CHAGRIN | 1 | 1 | | | | | | |
| (M. BROSSET) M. BROSSET, surgeon | 1 | | | | | | | |
| ( RAFLOT) RAFLOT, roofer | 1 | 1 | | | 2 | | | |
| ( La PIERRE) La PIERRE, hairdresser | 1 | 1 | 3 | | | | | |
| (DUPRE) DUPRE, joiner | 1 | 1 | 2 | 1 | 1 | | | |
| (BOURGUIGNON) BOURGUIGNON | | | | | | | | |
| (MARCHEATERRE) MARCHEATERRE | 1 | 1 | | | | | | |
| (XAVIER) XAVIER, free mulatto | | | | | | | | 1 |
| (ROTUREAU) ROTUREAU | 1 | 1 | | | | | | |
| (St. GERMAIN) Le NORMAND | 1 | | | | | | | |
| (BARRE) JEAN BAPTISTE BARRE | 1 | 1 | 2 | | | | | |
| (PARISIEN) LAUVERGUAT | 1 | 1 | 2 | | | | | |
| (LAUVERGUAT) BARRE | 1 | | | | | | | |
| (MARIE) MARIE, free negress | | | | | | | | |

A-32

| (Proprietor) and Inhabitant | M | W | C | O | NS | NC | IS | MU |
|---|---|---|---|---|---|---|---|---|
| (BRUNET) La CONTOIS | | 1 | 1 | | | | | |
| (FLACON) JEAN LOUIS MATE dit FLACON | 1 | 1 | 4 | | 3 | 1 | | |
| ( La ROCHE) La ROCHE, carpenter | 1 | 1 | 2 | | 1 | | | |
| ( AVIGNON) BEAUCOURT | 1 | | | | | | | |
| (Le MAIRE) | | | | | | | | |
| (VITRE) PAUL VITRE | 1 | 1 | | | | | | |
| (ANGEBAUD) ANGEBAUD, joiner | 1 | | | | | | | |
| (COMERCY) COMMERCY, knife maker | 1 | 1 | 1 | | | | | |
| ( La CROIX) | | | | | | | | |
| ( FRANCOEUR) FRANCOEUR, baker | 1 | 1 | | | | | | |
| ( M. HERPIN) M. HERPIN, commissioner for the company | 1 | | | | | | | |
| ( JEAN NELLE) JEAN NELLE , carpenter | 1 | | | | | | | |
| (MATE) MATE, .waggoner | 1 | 1 | | | | | | |

5. Facing the woods ( no street at that time, now Dauphine street).

| (JULIEN GAUTIER) JULIEN GAUTIER | 1 | | | | | | | |

A-32

| (Proprietor) and Inhabitant | M | W | C | O | NS | NC | IS | MU |
|---|---|---|---|---|---|---|---|---|
| (FAUCHE) | | | | | | | | |
| GUILLAUME FAUCHE | 1 | 1 | 1 | | | | | |
| NICOLAS VALET | 1 | | | | | | | |
| La COURTABLEAU ( woman) | | 1 | | | | | | |
| ( For the desceased NAUTIER) | | | | | | | | |
| (MENAGER) | | | | | | | | |
| MENAGER | 1 | 1 | | | | | | |
| MATHURIN | 1 | | | | | | | |
| ( M. LARCHE) | | | | | | | | |
| M. LARCHE | 1 | | | | | | | |
| CONTOIS | 1 | 1 | | | 3 | | | |
| LEBODET | 1 | | | | | | | |

6. Rue St. Philip ( St. Philip Street)

| | M | W | C | O | NS | NC | IS | MU |
|---|---|---|---|---|---|---|---|---|
| ( M. TRUDEAU) | | | | | | | | |
| Made. TRUDEAU | | 1 | 2 | | | | | |
| Mlle. TRUDEAU | | 1 | | | | | | |
| M. LAVAU | 1 | | | | | | | |
| ( M. DALCOURT) | | | | | | | | |
| (M. GAUVRIT) | | | | | | | | |
| (M. de St. MARTIN) | | | | | | | | |
| M. de St. MARTIN | 1 | | | | | | | |
| ( La ROSE) | | | | | | | | |
| La ROSE, waggoner | 1 | 1 | 1 | | | | | |
| (La PRAIRIE) | | | | | | | | |
| La PRAIRIE, bohemian | 1 | 1 | 1 | 1 | | | | |
| (GUIDOU) | | | | | | | | |
| GUIDOU | 1 | 1 | 2 | | | | | |
| widow FONDELAY | | 1 | | | | | | |
| (VINCENT) | | | | | | | | |
| VINCENT | 1 | 1 | | | | | | |

A-32

| ( Proprietor) and Inhabitant | M | W | C | O | NS | NC | IS | MU |
|---|---|---|---|---|---|---|---|---|
| ( M. St. MICHEL) | | | | | | | | |
| M. St. MICHEL | 1 | | | | | | | |

**7. Rue Dumaine ( Dumaine street)**

| | M | W | C | O | NS | NC | IS | MU |
|---|---|---|---|---|---|---|---|---|
| (BARRE) | | | | | | | | |
| CHENEAU, gunner | 1 | | | | | | | |
| (AMELIN) | | | | | | | | |
| AMELIN | 1 | 1 | | | | | 1 | |
| La BIGNARD (woman) | | | | | | | | |
| (MARIN) | | | | | | | | |
| MARIN | 1 | 1 | 2 | | | 1 | 1 | |
| (MEUNIER) | | | | | | | | |
| (BIGOT) | | | | | | | | |
| BIGOT | 1 | | | | 2 | | | |
| La AUBERT (woman) | | 1 | | | | | | |
| (M. BRUSLE) | | | | | | | | |
| M. BRUSLE, councillor | 1 | | 5 | | 5 | 6 | | |
| Made. BRUSLE | | 1 | | | | | | |

**8. Rue St. Anne ( St. Anne street)**

| | M | W | C | O | NS | NC | IS | MU |
|---|---|---|---|---|---|---|---|---|
| ( The king) | | | | | | | | |
| M. PERIER | 1 | | 3 | | 3 | 2 | 1 | |
| Made. PERIER | | 1 | | | | | | |
| Mlle. TERLIN | | 1 | | | | | | |
| M. Le MAITRE | 1 | | | | | | | |
| M. LABBE, boat owner | | | | | | | | |
| (THOMAS ASSELIN) | | | | | | | | |
| THOMAS ASSELIN | 1 | 1 | | | | | | |
| CATHERINNE HUBERT | | 1 | | | | | | |
| MARIE JEAN VIEL | | 1 | | | | | | |
| (DUPARC) | | | | | | | | |
| DUPARC, interpreter | 1 | 1 | 3 | | 4 | | | |
| (La MORY) | | | | | | | | |
| La MORY | | | | | | | | |

A-32

| (Proprietor) and<br>Inhabitant | M | W | C | O | NS | NC | IS | MU |
|---|---|---|---|---|---|---|---|---|
| (BOURBON)<br>BOURBON | 1 | 1 | | 1 | | | | |
| (JEAN LOUIS) | | | | | | | | |
| ( LAUVE)<br>LAUVE, tailor | 1 | 1 | 2 | | 1 | | | |
| (BRANTAU)<br>BRANTAU, gunsmith | 1 | | | | | | | |
| ( LOISEL)<br>ROMAYOUX, locksmith | 1 | 1 | 3 | | 1 | | | |
| ( BOURGUIGNON)<br>BOURGUIGNON | 1 | | | | | | | |
| ( JULLIEN)<br>JULLIAN | 1 | | | | | | | |
| (BUNEL)<br>BUNEL | 1 | 1 | 1 | 1 | 6 | | | |
| ( JARDELA)<br>JARDELA | 1 | 1 | 1 | | | | | |
| (BOTZON)<br>BOTZON, blacksmith | 1 | 1 | 1 | | 4 | | | |

9. Rue d'Orleans ( Orleans street)

| | M | W | C | O | NS | NC | IS | MU |
|---|---|---|---|---|---|---|---|---|
| ( JEAN LOUIS)<br>JEAN LOUIS, patron | 1 | | | 3 | 2 | 1 | | |
| ( La COSTE)<br>La COSTE, church warden | 1 | | | | | | | |
| (DARGAREY) | | | | | | | | |
| ( succession of SABANNIER)<br>PICQUARD | 1 | 1 | | | | | | |
| ( MARIE FRANCOISE)<br>MARIE FRANCOISE | | 1 | | | | | | |

A-32

| ( Proprietor) and Inhabitant | M | W | C | O | NS | NC | IS | MU |
|---|---|---|---|---|---|---|---|---|
| (BALLE) | | | | | | | | |
| BALLE, joiner | 1 | 1 | | | | | | |
| (DUBUISSON) | | | | | | | | |
| DUBUISSON | 1 | | | | | | | |
| (LAMBERT) | | | | | | | | |
| LAMBERT | 1 | | | | | | | |
| BELLAIR | 1 | | | | | | | |
| (VINCENT) | | | | | | | | |
| (GALOIRE) | | | | | | | | |
| GALOIRE | 1 | | | | | | | |
| NICOLAS  CARQUET dit PIPY | 1 | | | | | | | |
| ( M. DAUSSEVILLE) | | | | | | | | |
| M. GRACE, accountant for the hospital | 1 | | | | | | | |
| Made. GRACE | | 1 | | | | | | |

10. Rue St. Pierre ( St. Peter street)

| | M | W | C | O | NS | NC | IS | MU |
|---|---|---|---|---|---|---|---|---|
| ( Made. CHAMILLY) | | | | | | | | |
| Made, CHAMILLY | | | 1 | 2 | | 1 | 1 | |
| Mlle. St. MARTIN | | | | | | | | |
| Mlle. CHAMILLY ( marriagable girls) | | | | | | | | |
| (PINET) | | | | | | | | |
| PINET, gunsmith | 1 | 1 | | | | | | |
| (ANDRE ROCHER) | | | | | | | | |
| ANDRE ROCHER | 1 | 1 | | | | | | |
| SIMART, sailor | 1 | 1 | 1 | | | | | |
| RACQUETTE, patron | 1 | | | | | | | |
| (ROBERT) | | | | | | | | |
| ROBERT, sergeant | | 1 | 3 | | 1 | | | |
| (DURANTAY) | | | | | | | | |
| DURANTAY | 1 | | | | | 1 | 1 | |

A-32

| ( Proprietor) and Inhabitant | M | W | C | O | NS | NC | IS | MU |
|---|---|---|---|---|---|---|---|---|
| (JACOUILLON) | | | | | | | | |
| JACOUILLON,_former soldier | 1 | 1 | 4 | | | | | |
| (widow BAILLIF) | | | | | | | | |
| widow BAILLIF | | 1 | | | | | | |
| (AUBRUN) | | | | | | | | |
| AUBRUN, mason | 1 | | | | | | | |
| La DUPRE | | | | | | | | |
| (NEGRIER) | | | | | | | | |
| NEGRIER,_former foreman | 1 | 1 | | | 1 | | | |
| ROBERT, tailor | 1 | | | | | | | |
| (SKIL) | | | | | | | | |
| MARC SKIL | 1 | 1 | | | | | | |

11. Rue de Toulouze ( Toulouse street)

| | M | W | C | O | NS | NC | IS | MU |
|---|---|---|---|---|---|---|---|---|
| (TOURENJEAU) | | | | | | | | |
| TOURENJEAU, gardner | 1 | 1 | | | 1 | | | |
| ( FRANCOEUR) | | | | | | | | |
| ( La CHENAY) | | | | | | | | |
| La CHENAY, sieur De LONG | 1 | 1 | | | | | | |
| (TOURENJEAU) | | | | | | | | |
| LIGUY, carpenter | 1 | | | | | | | |
| widow DUCROS | | 1 | | | | | | |
| (FILASSIER) | | | | | | | | |
| FILASSIER, goldsmith | 1 | 1 | | | | | | |
| DAUVERGUE, goldsmith | 1 | | | | | | | |
| (AVIGNON) | | | | | | | | |
| AVIGNON | 1 | 1 | | | 1 | 1 | | |
| ( SANS FACON) | | | | | | | | |
| SANS FACON | 1 | | | | 2 | | | |
| (PIOZAT) | | | | | | | | |
| PIOZAT, hairdresser | 1 | | | | | | | |
| MILET, mason | 1 | 1 | | | | | | |

A-32

| ( Proprietor) and Inhabitant | M | W | C | O | NS | NC | IS | MU |
|---|---|---|---|---|---|---|---|---|
| (COUPARD) COUPARD, carpenter | 1 | 1 | | | 3 | 1 | | |
| ( M. MORISET) M. MORISET | 1 | 1 | 2 | | 3 | 1 | | |
| ( M. de LOUBOEY) M. de LOUBOEY, Kings Lieutenant | 1 | | | | 3 | 3 | | |
| ( M. ROSSARD) M. ROSSARD, attorney | 1 | | | | 4 | 1 | | 1 |
| 12. Rue Conti ( Conti street) ( M. de LERY) LOUIS GISCARD dit BENERIS | 1 | 1 | 1 | | 2 | | | |
| ( M. DAUSSEVILLE) | | | | | | | | |
| ( M. de MOUY) | | | | | | | | |
| ( DESLATTES) MICHEL DESLATTES | 1 | | | | | | | |
| DESLATTES, joiner | 1 | 1 | 1 | | | | | |
| ( the King) MARQUET, sail maker | 1 | 1 | | | | | | |
| ( M. SAROT) SAROT | 1 | | | | 1 | | | |
| (RICARD) RICARD | 1 | | | | | | | |
| LIOTAUR | 1 | | | | | | | |
| ( St. JACQUES) HERVE | 1 | | | | | | | |

13. Rue St. Louis ( St. Louis street)

| | M | W | C | O | NS | NC | IS | MU |
|---|---|---|---|---|---|---|---|---|
| (REITER) REITER | 1 | 1 | | 1 | 1 | | | |
| ( CRISTANA) CRISTANA | 1 | 1 | | | | | | |

A-32

| ( Proprietor) and Inhabitant | M | W | C | O | NS | NC | IS | MU |
|---|---|---|---|---|---|---|---|---|
| ( THOMAS LAGE) | | | | | | | | |
| THOMAS LAGE | 1 | 1 | 2 | | | | | |
| JEAN COSSET, marine carpenter | 1 | | | | | | | |
| (M.ALEXANDRE) | | | | | | | | |
| M. ALEXANDRE, surgeon for the Hospital | 1 | | 1 | | 6 | 1 | | |
| Made. ALEXANDRE | | 1 | | | | | | |
| ( Made. BOUPARD) | | | | | | | | |
| Made. BOUPARD | | 1 | | | 1 | | | |
| ( AUFRERE) | | | | | | | | |
| AUFRERE | 1 | 1 | 3 | | | | | 1 |
| (BELLEGARDE) | | | | | | | | |
| BELLEGARDE | 1 | 1 | 1 | | 5 | 1 | | |
| ( M. de la CHAISE) | | | | | | | | |
| M. de la CHAISE | 1 | | | | | 2 | | |
| M. DEBAT | 1 | | | | | | | |
| (DAUBLIN) | | | | | | | | |
| DAUBLIN, blacksmith | 1 | 1 | 1 | | 1 | | | |
| M. BRU, agent for the Company of the Indies | 1 | | | | 1 | 2 | | |

\* \* \* \* \* \* \* \* \* \*

LIST OF LANDOWNERS LOCATED ALONG THE
MISSISSIPPI RIVER FROM ITS MOUTH TO THE GERMAN VILLAGES
WITH INDICATIONS OF HOW THEY ACQUIRED THE LAND. After 1731

1. Starting just below New Orleans, and proceeding to the
mouth of the river. ( east bank)

| | |
|---|---|
| DREUX | by grant and from Sieur LAGARDE and sieur CHAVANNE |
| DARBY | from sieur CHAVANNE |
| CANTILLON | by grant and from sieur BANESSE |
| COUSTILLAS | by grant |
| La POMMERAY | from widow La BOULAY whom he married |
| TRUDEAU | by grant |
| GAUVRIT | purchased from ESTIENNE L'ANGLOIS |
| La CHAISE | purchased from succession of DUPUY PLANCHARD |
| DALCOURT | purchased from succession of Le BLANC |
| MARAIS DUPUIS | by grant |
| MARAIS de la TOUR | by grant |
| RAGUET | purchased from  the MARAIS |
| BROUTIN | purchased from widow MANDEVILLE whom he married |
| FLEURIAU | by grant and from Sieur MORAND |

JORY GIBERY dit St. MARTIN purchased from DREUX brothers
The Ursuline nuns by grant

| | |
|---|---|
| DAUSSEVILLE | by grant, from BERTRAND JAFFRE dit La LIBERTE and from TERREBONNE |
| DEMORIERE | by grant |

The Capuchin  fathers by grant
BERTRAND JAFFRE dit La LIBERTE by grant

| | |
|---|---|
| La PRADE | by possession and from JOSEPH GIRARDY |
| LOUBOYE | by grant |
| DESQUEIRAC | by grant |
| CHAPERON | purchased from ROCHON and from LARCHEVEQUE and by grant |

La LOIRE JOUSSET by grant

| | |
|---|---|
| BACHEMIN | purchased from sieur  MANADE and by grant |
| CHAMYLY | by grant |
| LEONARD | by grant |
| LIVETTE | purchased from desceased sieur SCHEPART ( probably de CHEPART) |
| MORISSET | purchased from JACQUES and ROMAIN ROFINAC |
| DALCOURT | by permission of the council |
| MASSY | purchased from sieur D'HAUTERIVE |

```
BRUSLE          by grant
BALCOURT        by grant and from D'ARTELLE
PERARBE dit TRACE MONTAGNE  by grant
FILLARD         by grant and purchased from PAQUIER
CHEVAL          by grant and purchased from NICOLAS NOISET
BROSSET         by grant
BOYER           and the desceased CLEIRE FONTAINE
                            by grant
TIXERAND        from the widow CARRIERE whom he married
                            and by grant
JOSEPH CARRIERE by grant
FRANCOIS CARRIERE  by grant
JACAUES CARRIERE  by grant
MEUNIER         purchased from L'ANGLOIS
widow SAUCIER by grant
RIVART( son)    by grant
TRUDOT (son)    by possession and from De LAYE
ARNAUD          by grant and by possession.
4 brothers SAUCIER by grant
L'EMPILEUR      by possession
LAMY            by possession
PAQUET, the tailor, purchased from the free negro named
                            JEAN BAPTISTE
ROUGOT          purchased from ARNAUD
ROBIN           from sieur DELOT whose daughter he married
ALEXANDRE, surgeon major, purchased from NICOLAS PROUEST
                            and from Sieur ESTIENNE
BUSSON          by grant
DRAPAUX         by grant
FRANCOIS CARRIERE purchased from LORRIN and from St.
                            JOSEPH and by possession
BEAUPRE         purchased from FRANCOIS TRIBOULOU
MONTIGUIE       by possession
LUNELLE         abandoned, he returned to France
CASTEL dit LILOIS abandoned
CLAUDE RENAUD dit AVIGNON by grant
FAUCHAUX dit FRANCOEUR by possession
LOUIS COLLETTE dit JOLY COEUR by possession
La LIBARDIERE by possession
ROBIN           purchased from GABRIELLE MARTIN
TRONQUIDY       by grant
GUILLAUME       by possession
NICOLAS FIZEAU by grant
FIOU, pilot at the Balize, by possession
MADRE           by possession
```

2. Starting directly opposite New Orleans and proceeding
to the mouth of the river.( west bank).

| | |
|---|---|
| The King | Property of the Company of the Indies forming a triangle at a point on the river ( Algiers point) |
| CHARLES BOURGEOIS | purchased from M. de BIENVILLE |
| M. de BIENVILLE | this concession granted by the company of the Indies |
| BALDIE | Purchased from AUBUCHON |
| PROVANCHEZ | by contract with M. de BIENVILLE |
| AUGUSTIN LANGLOIS | by contract with M. de BIENVILLE |
| RIVARD | purchased from the succession of PIERRE EMERY |
| ESTIENNE LANGLOIS | by contract with M. de BIENVILLE |
| LOUIS LANGLOIS | by permission of M. de BIENVILLE |
| RAGUET | by possession |
| JORY GUIBERRY dit St. MARTIN | from the widow DUGUAY whom he married, and who obtained the land from contract with M. de BIENVILLE and by grant |
| MICHEL VIENT | by grant |

(Note: The above land was all part of the original
concession granted to M. de BIENVILLE who is
in France when this item was compiled)

| | |
|---|---|
| TRUDOT and DALCOURT | purchased from BOURBOT and from PAUL ALLEMAND |
| BUQUOY dit PLAISANCE | by possession |
| BAULNE | purchased from M. FAZENDE in the name of M. PERRY |
| FAZENDE | by grant |
| DEMORIERE, widow, purchased from BOURBOT | |
| PELLERIN | purchased from sieur MASSY |
| CHAPERON | purchased from PROVANCHEZ |
| BARRE | purchased from sieur PRAT |
| COUSSINE | by grant |
| FLEURIE | purchased from BIGOT |
| AUBERT, widow, by grant | |
| GRASSE | by grant |
| DUMANOIR | purchased from sieur VEILLON |
| MARCILLY | from the widow TREPAGNIE whom he married |
| LABRO | from the widow BACHERRE whom he married |
| MARCILLY | by possession |
| JOSEPH CARRIERE | by grant |
| MEUNIER | by possession |
| TIXERAND | by grant |
| BROUTIN | by grant |

B-32

IGNACE TREPAGNIE  by grant
FRANCOIS TREPAGNIE  by grant
Concession of Saint Catherine by possession
D'ASFELD concession  by title
ROQUIGNIE        by grant
JACQUE PERRIER  by grant
MASSY           by grant and purchased from sieur ROSSARD
ROBIN           by possession
THOMELIN        purchased from LaCOSTE, JOYAUX, and CONSTANT


3. Starting above New Orleans at the city limits and on
the same side, proceeding upriver . ( east bank)

The jesuit priests, purchased from M. de BIENVILLE
D'HAUTERIVE    from the widow DUVAL whom he married and
                           by contract with M. de
                           BIENVILLE
VILLAINVILLE   This land is in estate, held by contract with
                           M. de BIENVILLE
DARBY          purchased from BERGERON and MALLO
BONNAUD        purchased from LARCHE LAINNEE
CARRIERE       purchased from the DAUPHIN family, father
                           and son
LIVAUDAIS      purchased from VIGIER
ROYE           purchased from HOUVRE, the german
VOISIN         purchased from sieur BUCHER
De BLANC       by contract with M. de BIENVILLE
PAQUIER        by contract with M. de BIENVILLE
Le SUEUR       by contract with M. de BIENVILLE
DEMOUYE        by contract with M. de BIENVILLE
BELLAIR        by contract with M. de BIENVILLE and pur-
                           chased from COUNE
BLANPAIN       purchased from JOSEPH CHAMIEE
CHAVANNE       purchased from La CHAISE, son, from
                           RODOLFE GUILLAIN and
                           contract with M. de
                           BIENVILLE
ADAM dit BLONDIN  by possession and purchased from
                           FRANÇOIS DONNE
PRADEL         purchased from sieur PREVOST
La FRENIERRE   by possession
De MOUYE       from the widow BEAULIEU whom he married
           ( Note: The above land was all part of the original
           concession granted to M. de BIENVILLE who is in
           France when this item was compiled)

                                        B-32

```
DUBREUIL VILLAR  concession
De LERY          succession by grant
De MOUYE         from the widow BAULIEU whom he married
La FRENIERRE  by grant and purchase from PIERRE CHAUVIN
The St. Reine concession  by grant, also purchased from
                 M. MASSY and M. GUENOT and from Sieur
                 DUBREUIL VILLAR
De LERY, oldest son, by grant
De LERY BOISELEIRE by grant
De LERY des ISLETS by grant
De LERY          succession and purchased from LOUIS DASLENNE
VERRETTE         by grant and purchase from HUGOT
BELLEVUE         by purchase from HUBERT DE LA CROIX and
                 JEAN HUBERT
La FRENIERE   by grant
BENAC            by grant and purchase from Sieur DEROCHE
d'ARTAGUIETTE major of the city ( New Orleans), by purchase
                 from VAQUIER, La PIERRE, and sieur PELLERIN
d'ARTAGUETTE  concession  by grant
d'ARTAGNANT   concession by grant
BENAC            purchased from DAUPHIN and from PUGEAU
ANDRE CRESPE  by grant and purchase from BENAC and from
                 JOSEPH ARASSE
JEAN BARRE dit LIONNOIS by grant
HUET dit DULUDE   purchased from CLAUDE MEIREAU
SANSON           by purchase from AUFRERE
YZET             by purchase from SANSON
ANTOINE ROYE dit La FLEUR  by purchase from FERANDON
YZET             by grant and purchase from MALABISE and from
                 FEUDERICE
ANTOINE          a sergeant, by possession
JEAN VEBURE   by possession
Du SABLE         by possession His land abandoned, he is now
                 at Chetimachas.
JOSEPH MARY   by purchase from Le MESLE dit BELLEGARDE
FRANCOIS Le MESLE dit BELLEGARDE  purchase from POUPART
                 dit La FLEUR and from POUDRET and by grant
                 This land is at Bustards ( Outardes)
LOUIS TOUBS   by possession
GASPARD TOUBS by purchase from  sieur GAULLAS
AMBROISE HEYDEL by possession and purchase from GAULLAS
JEAN VILLAR dit LIONNOIS by possession
HENRY HOTIAU and FERANDON by possession
PIERRE BROUE dit BELLODOT by possession
JACQUE SERIGNON by possession
d'OMOR dit DAUPHINE by possession
                                    B-32
```

LOUIS La CHAMPAGNE by possession
FRANCOIS CHEVAL by grant and purchase from DUBUISSON
JACQUE ANTOINE Le BORNE by possession
ANTOINNE BOUCHARANT by verbial permission
CHAMPIGNEUL    by grant
BOQUET         by purchase from HENRY HOTION and FERANDON
RENE d'ORVIN   by purchase from Le BORNE
PIERRE POMMIER  by grant
NICOLAS VIENER  by purchase from JACQUE PAUCHER
DANIEL POPF    by purchase from JOSEPH de KENTERECK
               dit DUPONT
ANDRE MASSE    by purchase from de KENTERICK dit DUPONT
               and from POPF and from LAVERGNE
ANTOINNE BOUCHARAND associate with LAMATIE by grant
PAUCHER dit La CHAPELLE by possession
JEAN BAPTISTE MONPIERRE by possession
JEAN LACOSTE   by grant
               This last entry is at the Colapissa village
               next to the concession of DANCENY which is
               at present abandoned.


4. Starting above New Orleans, across the river ( west bank)
and proceeding upriver from a point directly across from
the city.

PERIER         purchased from the succession of M. de
               PAILLOUX, from Sieur BIZOTON and by grant
La CHAISE      succession by grant
l'EMPILLEUR    by grant
LARCHE LAINNE  by purchase from ROYE and from La GOUBLAYE
JOSEPH LARCHE  by grant and purchase from LEMPILLEUR
BIMONT         from the widow RICHAUME whom he married
VIGIER         by grant
MALBOUROUCK    by purchase from MEUSLION
MAREILLY       by purchase from JUDICE
JUDICE         by possession and by permission of the council.
RIXNER         by purchase from SCHEMITTE
St. TERESE     by grant and purchased from M. de BOISBRIANT
BESLILE        by grant and purchased from CLAUDE BAILLY
LIVAUDAIS      by possession
SIMON          a mulatto, by possession and purchased from
               a free negro named SCIPION
GUEHOT         by possession
SENET          by purchase from BELLAIRE
DASFELD        concession at Petit Dezert

DEMOUYE          from the widow BAULIEU whom he married
MIKELLE          by purchase from  sieur DUBREUILLE VILLAR
DUBREUILLE VILLAR  concession
La FRENIERE      by grant and purchase from sieur MASSY
De LERY          succession by grant and purchase from MASSY
DEMOUYE          from the widow BAULIEU whom he married
PETIT LIVILLE by grant and purchased from  sieur TIERRY
COULLANGE        by grant and purchased from IMBERT
SENET            by grant
BAILLY           by grant
KERNION          by possession and purchase
LAVERGNE         a canadian by purchase from St. JULLIEN
St. JULLIEN      by title of possession
BARRON           by purchase from SENET. This property is
                 at the Oumas
SIMON CONNE      by grant and purchase from GASPART AYGUY
PUEGOL           by purchase from Le BAT and KERNION
NOYON            by grant and by possession
DARTAGUET        major at New Orleans  by grant
JACQUE BEAUSERGEANT  by possession
JACQUE DUPRE  by possession
HENRY CHRISTMAN  by possession
ANDRE CHRISTMAN  by possession
JACQUE CHRISTMAN by possession
WANDERECK        by possession
JACQUE NEYGUY  by possession
PHILIPE SONT  by possession
FRANCOIS DONNE  by possession
JACQUE CROISIEZ by possession
ROUSSEAU         by purchase from JACQUE DUPRE
JACQUE FOLTZ  by possession
ANDRE OFFEMANNE  by possession
CHRISTIANNE GRAINER  by possession
PIERRE CLEIROT  by possession
JEAN DESLANDE  by possession and purchase from LAVERGNE
LAVERGNE         by possession
GASPART AEICKLY  by possession
LABEE            by grant
MOREAU dit PARISIEN  by grant
DAVID MEUNIER by possession
LABEE            by grant  and by possession
St. TON          by grant. This place is opposite Bustard
                 ( Outardes).
JACQUE RABELLS  by possession
JACQUE VEISCRANNE  by possession

B-32

JEAN ADAM        by possession
GEORGE TROSLER   by possession
GEORGE ROEFER    by possession
JACQUE and CHRISTOFLE HOUBRE, father and son, by possession
BERNARD ANTOINNE  by possession
MATHIAS FREDERICK by possession
JOSEPHE WAGENSBACH by possession
De MEUVE         concession Some of this property is consigned
                 to the servant LeBARQUENT. All the land is
                 occupied along the river.
JEAN BAPTISTE BOURGEOIS by possession
ANDRE STUMPHLE   by possession
PIERRE MUNIQUE   by possession
CHRISTOFLE KAISER  by possession
SIMON BERLINGER  by possession
ADAM SCHEMITTE   by possession
JOSEPH ANDRE  by possession
Property of the Presbytery by possession
ANDRE DRACGUER  by possession
DARRANSBOURG  by grant
CLAUS MAYER      by possession
JACQUE RITTER by possession
ADAM MATERNE  by possession
LEONARD MAGDOLFE by possession
BALTAZAR MARIUS  by possession
ANDRE CHANTZE by possession
GUILLAUME CIRIAQUE  by possession
ALBERT SEGSNEIDER  by possession
BERNARD VIQUE  by possession
COURAT        by possession
JEAN ROMMELLE by possession
RODOLFE GUILLAND by possession
JEAN CALLENDRE by possession
JEAN GEORGE POQUE  by possession
MICHEL GAULLOIS dit LANGOUMOIS  by possession
MICHEL VOGUEL by possession
MARTIN LAMBERT by possession

The above landowners along the river acquired their possession by marriage to the widow of the previous owner, by
grant of the Company of the Indies, by permission of the
Superior council, by purchase from a previous owner, and
by possession, this last  implying that they were granted
title by nature of working the land  assigned to them in
lieu of their passage back to France ( especially the Germans formerly of the Law Arkansas concession).  This last
would be equivalent to "squatters rights".

B-32

## NOTES ON THE CENSUS FOR ILLINOIS, JANUARY 1732

Illinois was under the juristiction of Louisiana with government from New Orleans in the 1720's and 1730's. The census of the fort included Fort Chartres, Cascassias, Cahoquias, and the mines of M. Renault.

The census includes the following:

| | | |
|---|---|---|
| men | | 159 |
| women | | 39 |
| legitimate children | (LC) | 170 |
| natural children and orphans | (UC) | 20 |
| negroes and negresses belonging to the Company of the Indies | (NS) | 81 |
| Negro children, both sexes | (NC) | 64 |
| Indian slaves, both sexes | (IS) | 119 |
| Total of european descent | | 388 |
| Total others | | 264 |

The original of this census also includes totals and ownership of cattle, bulls and cows, horses, pigs,houses, mills, and stables.  It also gives the number of arpents of land assigned to each family.

The original is unsigned, but initialled by N.S., probably M. Salmon, who was ordinator for Louisiana when this census was taken.

## CENSUS OF THE INHABITANTS OF ILLINOIS DATED
JANUARY 1, 1732 ( Unsigned but initialled by N.S.)

| Inhabitant | LC | UC | NS | NC | IS |
|---|---|---|---|---|---|
| M de St. AGNE, senior officer and his wife | 2, | 0, | 0, | 0, | 6 |
| M. TERRISSE de TERNAY, officer | | 2, | 2, | 3 | |
| M de TONTI | | | | | |
| Le sieur HEBERT the elder and his wife | 1, | 0, | 3, | 4, | 3 |
| Le sieur NAULT | 1, | | | | |
| Le sieur FABUT ( SABUT?) | | | | | |
| Le sieur De LESSART, his wife | 3, | 1, | 3, | 2, | 5 |
| SANS CHAGRIN and his wife | 5, | 0, | 0, | 0, | 1 |
| BARON and his wife | 4, | | | | |
| NEUPORT and his wife | 1, | | | | |
| La PLUME | 1, | 1, | 2, | 2, | |
| BECQUET and his wife | 1, | 0, | 0, | 0, | 3 |
| HUBERT FINET and his wife | | | | | |
| PLACE, the notary | 0, | 1, | | | |

On the prairie of Fort Chartres of Illinois

| | LC | UC | NS | NC | IS |
|---|---|---|---|---|---|
| ROLLET and his wife | 2, | 0, | 0, | 0, | 1 |
| GOUVERNEUR and Le BRUN, associates | | | | | |
| BELHUMEUR and his wife | | | | | |
| DRAGON and his wife | 3, | | | | |
| the widow CHASSIN | 3, | 0, | 0, | 1, | 1 |
| FREDERIC, surgeon, and his wife | 4, | 0, | 0, | 0, | 1 |
| THOMAS | | | | | |
| LOUIS, the spaniard | | | | | |
| St. JEAN and his wife | 1, | 0, | 0, | 0, | 1 |
| BELLEROSE | | | | | |
| COUSSOL, soldier, and wife | 3, | | | | |
| DAUPHIN and his wife | 4, | | | | |
| La POINTE, ( Given to his son in law, La Roche) | | | | | |
| La ROCHE and his wife | 0, | 0, | 3, | | |
| TURPIN, the elder | 1, | 2, | | | |
| LOISEL and his wife | 1, | 0, | 2, | 3, | |
| HEBERT the younger and his wife | 1, | 0, | 0, | 0, | 2 |
| CLAUDE BAUNET and his wife | 3, | | | | |
| PICHARD | 0, | 1, | | | |
| GEROSINE and his wife | 1, | 2, | | | |
| GROS JEAN of New Orleans | | | | | |

C -32

| | LC | UC | NS | NC | IS |
|---|---|---|---|---|---|
| LANGEVIN and his wife | 2, | | | | |
| ROBILLARD and his wife | 1, | | | | |
| BACANET and his wife | 1, | | | | |
| BEAUSEJOUR | | | | | |
| PANERACE and his wife | 3, | | | | |
| HENRION and his wife | 3, | | | | |
| The widow PRE | 2, | | | | |
| St, PIERRE La VERDURE and his.wife | 1, | | | | |
| GOSSIAU and his wife, at the rock prairie | 1, | 0, | 1, | | |
| La LANDE the younger and his wife at the big prairie | 3, | 0, | 2, | 4, | 5 |

Inhabitants of Cacassias in Illinois

| | LC | UC | NS | NC | IS |
|---|---|---|---|---|---|
| The reverend Jesuit priests | 0, | 3, | 14, | 8, | 3 |
| Le sieur CARRIERRE and his wife | 1, | 0, | 6, | 9, | |
| Du LONGPRE and his wife | 1, | 1, | 3, | 2, | 3 |
| MICHEL PHILIPPES | 3, | 2, | 4, | 2, | 2 |
| COLLET | | | | | |
| La SOURCE and his wife | 4, | 1, | 4, | 4, | 4 |
| TURPIN and his wife | 5, | 1, | 4, | 1, | 2 |
| La ROSE and his wife | 4, | | | | |
| BLOT and his wife | 0, | 0, | 3, | 0, | 3 |
| La FATIGUE and his wife | 5, | 0, | 0, | 1, | 1 |
| PORTIER and his wife | | | | | |
| Le MOINE and his wife | 4, | | | | |
| La SONDE and his wife | 5, | 1, | | | |
| POTIER and his wife | 8, | 0, | 1, | 1, | 2 |
| La RIGUEUR and his wife | 0, | 1, | 0, | 0, | 3 |
| De VIGUES and his wife | 4, | 2, | 5, | 5, | 1 |
| AUBUCHON and his wife | 3, | 0, | 2, | 0, | 1 |
| BIENVENU and his wife | 4, | 0, | 1, | 0, | 4 |
| CRELY and his wife | | | | | |
| Du FRESNE and his wife | 0, | 0, | 0, | 0, | 1 |
| SANS REGRET and his wife | 0, | 0, | 0, | 0, | 1 |
| La LANDE the elder and his wife | 3, | 0, | 2, | 0, | 4 |
| St. PIERRE and his wife | | | | | |
| The land belonged to the desceased M. MELIQUE | 2, | 0, | 0, | 0, | 2 |
| Des LAURIERS | 0, | 1, | | | |
| BEAUVAIS and his wife | 4, | 0, | 2, | 0, | 2 |
| Le GRAS and his wife | 4, | 0, | 0, | 0, | 2 |
| St. YVES and his wife | 0, | 0, | 0, | 0, | 1 |
| QUENEL and his wife | 3, | 0, | 1, | 2 | |
| La FLEUR and his wife | 1, | | | | |

0-32

|  | LC | UC | NS | NC | IS |
|---|---|---|---|---|---|
| DE NOYONS | 0, | 0, | 0, | 0, | 1 |
| St. CERNAY |  |  |  |  |  |
| M. du TISNE, officer, his wife | 3, | 0, | 3, | 1, |  |
| VERRIER and his wife |  |  |  |  |  |
| St. JEAN and his wife | 3, |  |  |  |  |
| GLINEL and his wife | 3, | 0, | 0, | 0, | 1 |
| CHARRON and his wife | 2, | 1, | 1, |  |  |
| BAILLARGEON and his wife | 1, | 0, | 2, | 2, | 5 |
| DULUDE and LIBERGE, boy smiths |  |  |  |  |  |
| St YVES the elder and wife | 2, |  |  |  |  |
| ANTOINE the spaniard |  |  |  |  |  |
| OLIVIER and his wife | 3, | 0, | 0, | 0, | 1 |
| BOISJOLY, military captain | 0, | 0, | 0, | 0, | 1 |
| BOURBONNOIS and his wife | 0, | 0, | 0, | 0, | 4 |
| ALARD and his wife | 0, | 0, | 0, | 0, | 3 |
| La VIGNE and his wife | 2, | 0, | 0, | 0, | 1 |
| COURVILLE, tenant on the land of M. TESSIER | 0, | 0, | 2, | 4, | 4 |
| VALADON |  |  |  |  |  |

Mission of Cahoquias

| | LC | UC | NS | NC | IS |
|---|---|---|---|---|---|
| Made. MERCIER, superior and COURRIER, missionary |  |  | 4, | 0, | 4 |
| M. le MIEUX, and FLAMENT, engagee |  |  |  |  |  |
| LOUIS GAUT, habitant | 2, | 0, | 2, | 0, | 6 |
| CAPUCIN, habitant | 1, | 0, | 1, | 0, | 3 |
| La SOURCE, habitant | 1, | 0, | 1, |  |  |

Concession of M. RENAULT ( at his mine)

| | LC | UC | NS | NC | IS |
|---|---|---|---|---|---|
| M. RENAULT, director | 0, | 0, | 17, | 5 |  |
| RENAULT sons |  |  |  |  |  |
| La CROIX, father, his wife | 3, |  |  |  |  |
| La CROIX, son |  |  |  |  |  |
| MERCIER and his wife | 3, | 0, | 0, | 0, | 1 |
| M. du TISNE |  |  |  |  |  |
| QUEVEDO, the spaniard | 5, | . |  |  |  |

Mr REYNAULT at Illinois, his concession

| | LC | UC | NS | NC | IS |
|---|---|---|---|---|---|
| BOSSET | 2, |  |  |  |  |
| BLONDIN |  |  |  |  |  |
| GUEVREMONT and his wife | 1, |  |  |  |  |
| GERMAIN | 2, |  |  |  |  |
| POULAIN |  |  |  |  |  |
| La RAMEE | 1, |  |  |  |  |

C -32

# INDEX

www.ingramcontent.com/pod-product-compliance
Lightning Source LLC
Chambersburg PA
CBHW061737270326
41928CB00011B/2277

9 780806 304908